Your College Admissions Game Plan

50+ tips, strategies, and essential checklists for a winning college application for 9th, 10th, 11th, and 12th Graders

Related Titles for College-Bound Students

Dr. Jekyll and Mr. Hyde:
A Kaplan SAT Score-Raising Classic

Frankenstein: A Kaplan SAT Score-Raising Classic

The Scarlet Letter: A Kaplan SAT Score-Raising Classic

The Tales of Edgar Allan Poe:
A Kaplan SAT Score-Raising Classic

War of the Worlds: A Kaplan SAT Score-Raising Classic

Wuthering Heights: A Kaplan SAT Score-Raising Classic

Scholarships

You're Accepted

ACT Premier

ACT Strategies, Practice, and Review

ACT Strategies for Super Busy Students

ACT in a Box

SAT 2400

SAT in a Box

SAT Flashcards

SAT Strategies, Practice, and Review

SAT Strategies for Super Busy Students

12 Practice Tests for the SAT

AP Biology

AP Calculus AB & BC

AP Chemistry

AP English Language and Composition

AP English Literature and Composition

AP Environmental Science

AP Human Geography

AP U.S. Government & Politics

AP U.S. History

AP World History

SAT Subject Test: Mathematics Level 1

SAT Subject Test: Mathematics Level 2

SAT Subject Test: Physics

SAT Subject Test: Spanish

Your College Admissions Game Plan

50+ tips, strategies, and essential checklists for a winning college application for 9th, 10th, 11th, and 12th Graders

KAPLAN PUBLISHING

New York

© 2013 Kaplan, Inc.

Published by Kaplan Publishing, a division of Kaplan, Inc.
395 Hudson St,
New York, NY 10014

Printed in the United States of America

10 9 8 7 6 5 4 3

ISBN-13: 978-1-61865-291-1

For more information or to purchase books, please call the Simon & Schuster special sales department at 866-506-1949. If this is a rush order, call: 1(877) 989-0009.

Contents

Chapter 2: **Grade 9**

Chapter 3: **Grade 10**

Chapter 4: **Grade 11**

Chapter 5: **Grade 12**

Chapter 6: **Social Media and College Admissions**

Foreword

There's no doubt that the college admissions process is more stressful than ever. Not only do you need to be at the top of your game gradewise, these days you've got to "make your mark" in high school, too. You probably have tons of people telling you that you have to distinguish yourself—whether it's as captain of the football team, student body president, a concert pianist, or valedictorian—just to get noticed by your top colleges . . . all while holding down a part-time job, too. Oh, and don't forget those perfect SAT and ACT scores!

Seems impossible, right? Well, Kaplan is here to make it a little easier for you. *From Here to Freshman Year* gives you the step-by-step scoop on making sure you get through high school with everything you need to get into the college you want . . . without going crazy in the process.

Checklists for each year of high school give you an overview of what you should be thinking about and staying on top of.

Tips from real students guide you through the application process—it's like getting advice from a friend who's been through it already.

Our resource lists can point you to websites and books to learn more about homework help, volunteering, or anything else that you need more information about.

And remember, you don't have to run yourself into the ground trying to become a well-rounded overachiever—not when you already have the insider's tools to become the perfect college applicant.

Good luck!

Chapter 1:
Your Four-Year Plan

Quotes from Students Who've Been There, Done That

"I was so overwhelmed by how different everything in high school was that I wasn't even thinking about 10th or 11th grade. I did OK academically that year, but I wish I had been calmer and paid more attention to where I was going."

—Leo, 11th grade

"One thing I would tell a friend is to make sure you always leave some room for classes you like. I tried to take as many required courses as I could when I started high school, and it was miserable. Now I always leave room for an art class, or something else that I really enjoy, to balance out all the other stuff that I am not crazy about but I have to do anyway."

—Colin, 12th grade

"If you are getting behind in a class, get help with it sooner, not later! You can dig yourself into such a big hole by letting things pile up."

Aesha, 10th grade

"Studying with my friends really helped me with the transition into some of the harder classes in high school. Plus, then I didn't have to choose between doing homework and hanging out with my friends."

—Matt, 12th grade

"My guidance counselor told me it was important to show extra-curricular interests throughout all four years, not just at the end of high school, so I ran for student council and joined a club during my sophomore year."

—Melissa, 11th grade

"Taking AP classes, even just one a semester, really made my record a lot stronger when it was time to apply to colleges."

—Kaela, college freshman

Talking to Your Guidance Counselor

Think about this for a sec. How far would Harry Potter have gotten without Dumbledore? Or Frodo without Gandalf? Or King Arthur without Merlin?

You are about to embark on a great adventure, and like all great adventurers, you need two things—guidance and counsel. And whaddya know? Your guidance counselor is there to help you in just the same way.

So where do you start? Find out who your assigned counselor is and introduce yourself. A little shy? If you feel a little uncomfortable going into an unfamiliar person's office to say hi, prepare what you want to talk about so you have something to say after the initial "Hi, my name is Joe." Or, you can find out who your counselor is through your school's web site, and send them a friendly introductory email.

Some issues your guidance counselor can help you with in grade 9 are planning a high school career full of fun and challenging course work, discovering where your interests and talents lie, and keeping you on track for upcoming standardized tests.

Talking to an Independent Consultant

An independent consultant does a job similar to your guidance counselor for a fee.

Some specialize in opportunities for students with learning disabilities, student athletes, students considering medical school, and students with less-than-stellar test scores. They also offer guidance through every step of the application process and insider info about how colleges will view your application.

If you are considering this option, there are certainly some big plusses. They will give you major attention and individualized college advice in a comfortable, informal setting and during flexible hours. Some consultants also offer test-prep services in addition to counseling.

However, where they are different from your high school's guidance counselor is that they do not have a day-to-day perspective on how you act in a school or classroom environment. And again, independent consultants cost money. The fee can vary from a hundred bucks to a few thousand.

If you do decide to contact one, remember that qualifications vary a lot. Research and get references before you hire one. Also important to note is that it is an unethical (and illegal) practice for a consultant to promise you that you'll get accepted to a particular school or to write a college essay for you. If a consultant offers you either of these things, RUN!

Planning Your Course Load

We know what you're thinking—you've got to get used to a new school, make new friends, and meet new teachers. You don't know what you want to eat for lunch, let alone where you want to be after you graduate or what you have to do to get there! Don't worry—we're here to help.

Here's what most highly competitive colleges and universities are looking for academically from their applicants. You'll want to try to have these on your transcript:

- Four years of English
- Four years of math
- Four years of science
- Four years of social studies
- Three years of a single foreign language
- Two years of fine arts or performing arts
- One year (or more) of computers

Honors Classes and Advanced Placement

Most competitive colleges want students who not only do well, but also do well in challenging classes. With the help of your parents and guidance counselor, consider some of the following options:

- Taking honors or advanced placement (AP) courses instead of regular classes
- Taking four years of a single foreign language
- Taking four years of math instead of three
- Taking science classes that require lab work

Honors and AP classes are tougher than regular classes, but don't let the fear of a lower GPA stop you. Many selective colleges give difficult course work more weight than the easy stuff. For example, scoring high on AP exams can boost your academic profile and allow you to receive college credit for courses in those subjects. Receiving college credit means that while everyone else is forced to take a bunch of boring, easy introductory classes in the first semester, you get to skip those and dive right into the interesting, challenging classes you've been looking forward to instead!

Advanced Placement

In advanced placement (AP) classes, you improve your reading, reasoning, and writing skills. The College Board is responsible for administering exams that correspond with AP courses.

High scores in AP classes demonstrate mastery of college-level material, so admissions officers often attach a lot of weight to AP course work and exams. AP work could just give you the added edge over students with similar GPAs and admission test scores. Collegeboard.org now offers a search engine that allows you to look up specific institutions' policies on AP credit and placement.

But the exams are just the last step in a long process. It is strongly recommended that you take your high school's AP course if you plan to take the exam. Courses are typically taken in your junior or senior year. Your teacher or guidance counselor should have this information. Ask your teacher or guidance counselor for more information on AP courses at your school. Here is a list of the courses out there:

- Art History
- Biology
- Calculus AB
- Calculus BC
- Chemistry
- Chinese Language and Culture
- Comparative Government & Politics
- Computer Science A
- English Language and Composition
- English Literature and Composition
- Environmental Science
- European History
- French Language and Culture
- German Language and Culture
- Human Geography
- Italian Language and Culture
- Japanese Language and Culture
- Latin
- Macroeconomics
- Microeconomics
- Music Theory
- Physics B
- Physics C
- Psychology
- Spanish Language
- Spanish Literature and Culture
- Statistics
- Studio Art
- U.S. Government & Politics
- U.S. History
- World History

Great scores on AP exams can give you an edge in the college admissions process, and you can earn credit at most of the nation's universities and colleges. But which AP courses should you take? Should you take honors courses at all? Read on!

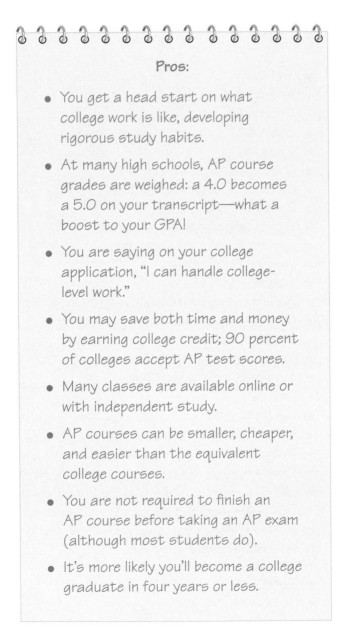

Pros:

- You get a head start on what college work is like, developing rigorous study habits.

- At many high schools, AP course grades are weighed: a 4.0 becomes a 5.0 on your transcript—what a boost to your GPA!

- You are saying on your college application, "I can handle college-level work."

- You may save both time and money by earning college credit; 90 percent of colleges accept AP test scores.

- Many classes are available online or with independent study.

- AP courses can be smaller, cheaper, and easier than the equivalent college courses.

- You are not required to finish an AP course before taking an AP exam (although most students do).

- It's more likely you'll become a college graduate in four years or less.

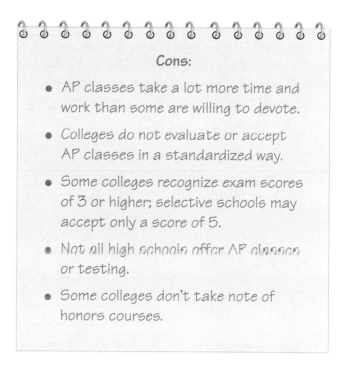

Cons:

- AP classes take a lot more time and work than some are willing to devote.

- Colleges do not evaluate or accept AP classes in a standardized way.

- Some colleges recognize exam scores of 3 or higher; selective schools may accept only a score of 5.

- Not all high schools offer AP classes or testing.

- Some colleges don't take note of honors courses.

AP Trivia!

On average, more than 2 million students from 15,000 high schools across the country take AP exams every year! The most popular exams include U.S. History, English Language and Composition, and English Literature and Composition.

The bottom line is that if you think that honors classes are for you, consider taking courses in subjects in which you are strong in, or you think you'll perform the best. And of course, talk to your guidance counselor for help on figuring out how to proceed. There is no need for you to work this out on your own! For more info on AP preparation options, visit *www.kaptest.com* or *www.collegeboard.org*.

Grades versus Test Scores

The people who hold your college fate in their hands have a method to ranking applications, and while this may surprise you, grades and the quality of your courses are more important than your SAT or ACT scores. Here's the scoop:

Really, really, really, really important:	GPA/Class Rank/ Course Work
Really, really, really important:	SAT/ACT Score
Really, really important:	Essays
Really important:	Teacher Recommendations
Important:	Extracurricular Activities

Now that you know, use this info to your advantage! You can do this throughout your high school career by:

- Forming good study habits early and setting the academic bar high
- Doing all you can to be prepared for the SAT/ACT
- Developing your writing skills and taking the college essay seriously
- Fostering positive relationships with teachers early
- Being involved in extracurricular activities that you love
- Volunteering your time to a cause that is important to you

A Note on Class Rank

Colleges view a high class rank as a strong indicator of academic potential. If your high school does rank its students, keep those grades up!

If your high school doesn't rank students, don't worry—colleges won't hold it against you. Either way, maintaining a good GPA is a sure way to win points with the admissions committee.

Beyond the Classroom

Colleges don't want kids who join every club, do every sport, and play every musical instrument on the face of the earth. Admissions officers are looking to create an invigorating campus environment with a well-rounded student body. They are looking for highly motivated students who invest their time and effort in their true passions, not people who do extracurricular activities just because they'll look good on a college application.

If you aren't excited about what you're doing, chances are you won't perform well and will either quit or be miserable. Besides, once you have that interview with Joe Admissions Officer, he'll totally know you weren't into that botany club you've been in since freshman year or the school newspaper you joined in sophomore year. The important thing is to do the things you love to do!

So grab a pen and paper and make a list of your interests. Then do your best to find extracurricular activities that match them. And before joining a club or activity, ask yourself:

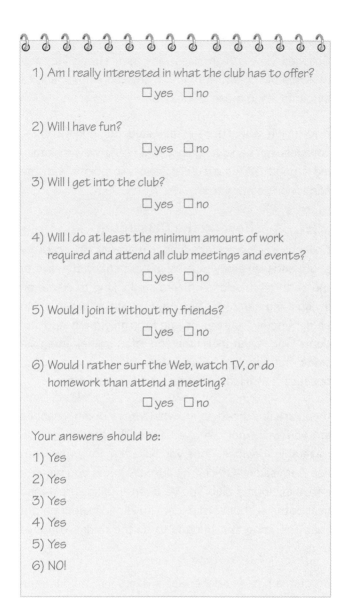

1) Am I really interested in what the club has to offer?

☐ yes ☐ no

2) Will I have fun?

☐ yes ☐ no

3) Will I get into the club?

☐ yes ☐ no

4) Will I do at least the minimum amount of work required and attend all club meetings and events?

☐ yes ☐ no

5) Would I join it without my friends?

☐ yes ☐ no

6) Would I rather surf the Web, watch TV, or do homework than attend a meeting?

☐ yes ☐ no

Your answers should be:

1) Yes

2) Yes

3) Yes

4) Yes

5) Yes

6) NO!

Common Questions about Extracurriculars

We know you want the perfect extracurriculars to go along with all the hard work you are putting into your classes. The "what if" scenarios below are some common situations that students just like you grapple with as they try to find that perfect experience.

Q. WHAT IF I find a club on the subject or activity that I love, but my school's club doesn't live up to my expectations?

A. Say the Young Scientists Club meets once a month to talk about beakers when you'd rather be conducting research and doing real experiments. Don't be afraid to talk to the club's president or advisor to suggest ways to improve the organization. If your suggestions fall on deaf ears, it's OK to respectfully bow out and move on. See if you can create a new club at school. Wouldn't that look great on your college applications?

You can also talk to your parents about participating in activities outside of school. Research what is being offered by individuals (like music tutors), private businesses (like dance or martial arts schools), or other organizations (like the YMCA or local community college) in your area. Talk to friends and relatives or your guidance counselor; they might have some great recommendations. And don't let a tight financial situation at home get you down. You will be able to find great activities you can participate in for free or little cost.

Q. WHAT IF I really, REALLY love solving quadratic equations and belong only to the math club?

A. No problem. A lot of passion and dedication in this one activity looks way better on your application than halfhearted involvement in other ones. Hey, you might even be a Fields Medal–winning mathematician some day!

Q. WHAT IF my only extracurriculars are several sports teams? I'm on the basketball, baseball, and wrestling teams, and I love all three! Do I have to pick just one?

A. Keep doing what you love! Your ability to do well on all three teams will show the admissions officers what your passions are and that you are dedicated and disciplined. What could be better for your applications?

Q. WHAT IF I sample lots of different clubs my freshman and sophomore years, then continue on with only one or two?

A. No one's going to hold that against you. You just had to figure out what you like, that's all!

Whatever you do, don't give up, ask for help when you're not sure how to move forward, and do what you love!

Volunteering

Volunteer Your Time for a Worthwhile Cause

Volunteering is a fantastic extracurricular activity. It will not only give you a great deal of satisfaction and self-respect to help people in need, it'll show you what it's like to work in the real world; and hey, it might even lead to a scholarship or turn into a job opportunity someday!

But don't just volunteer for any ol' cause. The "do what you love" rule applies here, too. For example: Are you totally into DIY (Do It Yourself) projects? Maybe you can build a house with Habitat for Humanity. Are sweet, furry creatures your thing? You might want to volunteer at a local animal shelter.

Get Started Volunteering To-Dos

Follow these steps to find a rewarding opportunity that's a great fit for your interests and your life:

✓ Narrow it down.
   First, take a look at the issues that affect your community: Shelters or soup kitchens are always in need of volunteers. If public schools aren't very well funded, maybe a local elementary school could use your help. Next, think about volunteering in relation to your other activities. It's a great way to add variety to your high school experience. For example, say you're on three sports teams and you volunteer coaching Little League, too. Of course, that's a great way to use your talents to help others. But you might want to consider other fields, like giving tours in an art museum or working with elders at a community center.

   And finally, if there's a field that you think might interest you as a career down the line, volunteering is a great way to get an inside look at the profession, meet people in the field who can serve as mentors, and gain some practical experience all at once.

✓ Make a list.
   When you have a sense of what kind of work you're interested in doing, do some research to determine where you will find opportunities. You might try:

   o *Getting involved in a volunteer group at school*
   o *Networking through family members or friends who volunteer or know people in the field*

- ○ *Searching the Internet to connect with one of the thousands of worthy causes (See page 15 for more info.)*
- ○ *Investigating opportunities with organizations like the United Way, your local YMCA, hospitals, your place of worship, or Girl/Boy Scouts*
- ○ *Starting your OWN volunteer program*
- ○ *Participating in specific events like a March of Dimes Walk or a 5K run for breast cancer*

✓ Make a plan.

Before you contact an organization, you should have a good idea of what you want your experience there to look like. What kind of work are you specifically interested in doing? Are there projects or areas you'd prefer to avoid?

Most importantly, take a realistic look at your schedule and other commitments. How much time can you commit to volunteering each week or month? It's better to err on the low side; you can always volunteer some extra hours, but you should avoid putting yourself in the position of having to cut back on your volunteer time.

✓ Get in touch.

When you've narrowed down your choices, it's time to contact the organization that you'd like to volunteer with. On a website, look for a "volunteer coordinator" or similar title. On the phone, just ask for the person who hires and trains volunteers. A phone call or email is a fine way to make the first contact—no need to send a formal letter. You'll want to introduce yourself, explain your interest in volunteering, and give a brief overview of what you'd like to do and how often.

*Be sure to present yourself profes-
sionally: return calls on time, check your
emails for spelling errors, and be friendly and
respectful. If you go for an in-person meeting, make sure to be on time, dress profes-
sionally, and smile. These seem like obvious
points, but they will make all the difference in
helping you to get off on the right foot.*

Volunteer Websites

If you already know a particular organization for which
you'd like to volunteer, find their website and take a
look. Most will have a page that provides contact and
other general information, and will be glad to hear from
you. If you're not quite that focused yet, here's a list of
websites that can help steer you in the right direction.
Good luck!

- VolunteerMatch (*www.volunteermatch.com*):
  At VolunteerMatch, you can search for volunteer openings in or near your town, for a specific age group, or within a particular field. You'll
  find listings from national and international
  nonprofits like Habitat for Humanity and the
  Peace Corps, as well as openings at smaller
  agencies that are unique to your area—over
  50,000 organizations in all! When you find a
  listing that interests you, just register and the
  site will send an email to the organization on
  your behalf.

- Network for Good (*www.networkforgood.org/
  volunteer*): Network for Good offers a similarly
  rich array of volunteer options, with some great
  extras: You can use their Volunteer Record of
  Service to track your volunteer hours and your
  thoughts on the experience. And a partnership
  with the United Nations allows you to do good
  from the comfort of your own home; if you

participate in the Online Volunteering Service, you'll be connected with one of hundreds of organizations that need your help.

- Idealist (*www.idealist.org*): Idealist provides a huge trove of volunteer opportunities with an international bent.

- Volunteer.gov (*www.volunteer.gov/gov*): This is a great site to check out openings for volunteer work at national parks, historic sites, and other public agencies.

Quality AND Quantity

Doing one walk in your senior year doesn't say much about you or your passions. It also shows admissions officers that you don't have a lot of enthusiasm or discipline.

When you find causes or activities that you love, try to spend a significant amount of time dedicated to them. That means months or years of going to meetings, participating in events—doing whatever it takes for you to really be involved. Besides, the more time and effort you devote to an organization, the more likely it is that your responsibilities can increase. You might be put in charge of planning events instead of just going to them. Or you could become a team manager or a summer camp leader. That kind of experience will be really valuable as you move from high school to college, and then on to the real world. Plus, admissions officers will be really impressed.

Document Your Experiences

It's important to keep a record of the time you spend volunteering—it can help you to apply for scholarships and jobs and maybe even to get school credit. You can do this in a notebook or journal, if that's most comfortable. Or if you prefer to keep an electronic record, a private blog or a basic word processing file is a simple way to keep your thoughts in one place. Your annotations can be very simple, like:

> Sallybrook Retirement Home
> June 2013–August 2013; five hours a week
>
> Responsibilities included general office tasks, lending a helping hand to busy nurses, and helping organize events like the Valentine's Day dinner/dance, the Fourth of July picnic, and bingo nights.
>
> New York Cares
> January–December 2013
>
> Participated in six urban renewal projects: painted murals, helped with a park cleanup, and attended fund-raisers that included a bake sale, a basketball tournament, and a hip-hop dance competition.

You can also track your hours at the Presidential Service Awards website, *www.presidentialserviceawards.gov*. This tracker will automatically add up recurring hours, such as a weekly volunteer commitment, so it's easy to see where you stand.

On top of counting your hours and making a list of tasks, consider keeping a record of the experience itself. What is volunteering like for you? What do you see or experience that is new to you? How does it make you think differently about your own life? What do you most enjoy about it, and what is most challenging? Thinking about your experience, and having a sense of how it affects you, will give you an edge when it comes time to talk about it with a potential boss, a teacher, or a college admissions counselor.

Scholarships

As you have probably noticed by now, there are a lot of things you can do in your freshman year of high school to help you get to your freshman year of college. Paying for college is definitely something that is never too early to start thinking about.

Don't let seemingly impossible tuition costs stop you from applying to college! There are plenty of financing opportunities out there to help you or your parents pay for school, and one of the best options is the college scholarship.

Types of Scholarships

Generally, scholarships and fellowships are reserved for students with special qualifications, such as academic, athletic, or artistic talent. However, there are awards out there for students who are interested in particular fields of study, who are members of underrepresented groups, who live in certain areas of the country, or who demonstrate financial need.

The most well-known sources for scholarships are, of course, colleges and universities. However, there are hundreds of sources that award money based on a wide variety of factors, including career plans, writing ability, research skills, religious or ethnic background, military or organizational activities, athletic success, personal characteristics, and even pure luck in random drawings. These sources include private companies, unions, professional organizations, clubs, lodges, foundations, and local and state governments.

Some state education authorities and other state agencies offer assistance above and beyond the usual tuition assistance programs. Some states also offer aid for particular fields of study to residents of the state who remain in-state to complete their studies.

How to Find Scholarships

There are a number of sources of aid to consider. Some may be obscure, while others may be quite obvious to you.

Start with your family! Ask your parents to check with their employers regarding available scholarship opportunities. Also, many scholarships from private employers can be awarded to people other than sons or daughters. Ask all your family members to check out the possibilities at their jobs!

Next up, your guidance counselor. He or she will be ready and able to answer any questions you might have and to help you start your search. For example, many high school guidance offices have a list of scholarships that have been secured by former students. These scholarships are often provided by local agencies that lack the resources to publicize them in other ways.

Books

There are many scholarship books out there. While they all contain extensive lists of scholarships, no book can be totally inclusive. Plus, a lot of them have "filler" scholarships that may be worth less than $100. While any free money you can get your hands on for college is good, you will have to be careful that you don't waste your time and money chasing scholarships that will hardly put a dent in your overall college cost burden.

Therefore, as with any research project, you should not depend on only one source. Multiple sources will yield the most extensive data and thus the most scholarship dollars. Some helpful books on scholarships include:

- *Kaplan Scholarships*, by Kaplan Publishing and Admissions: Packed with data compiled by Reference Service Press—the leading authority on scholarship sources—*Kaplan Scholarships* is an excellent one-stop resource. In addition, it is the only book that features more than 3,000 scholarships that are all worth at least $1,000, are not restricted to any one school, and do not require repayment of any kind.

- *How to Go to College Almost for Free,* by Ben Kaplan: After applying for and receiving more than $90,000 worth of scholarship money during high school, Ben Kaplan graduated magna cum laude from Harvard. Then he wrote and self-published this book to help other people achieve their college dreams. There's info on finding and applying to scholarships, as well as how to handle interviews.

- *The Scholarship Handbook*, by The College Board: Written by the nonprofit membership organization that administers the PSAT, SAT, and AP exams, among others. Includes information on scholarship, internship, and loan programs offered by foundations, charitable organizations, and state and federal government agencies.

There is usually a scholarship section in the reference room of any public library. Many of these books focus exclusively on particular types of scholarships for majors/grade levels, etc., saving you time you would otherwise spend reading fruitlessly.

Having family members look through the same books you're reading will allow you to compare lists and eliminate duplicates. You can also do group searches with friends. Don't let the possibility of your friends applying for the same scholarships prevent you from doing this! Most scholarships offer more than one award, and having more eyes search the same books will reduce the chance of overlooking resources.

Electronic Resources

Students are increasingly turning to the Internet for scholarship searches. The great advantage of using the Internet is that the information is right there at your fingertips, and searching online is less labor intensive than using books. And in some cases, you can apply online for scholarships.

The problem with searching online? You can't just open up any old search engine, type in "scholarships," and expect to find everything you need. Therefore, you'll need to search for scholarship databases. The good news is that the database can match details about you with criteria in the database faster than you can, saving valuable time. The bad news? Although you should be able to find exclusive listings in each database, there's a good deal of overlap among databases.

So if you go the online route, search a number of databases and then eliminate duplicates by checking the application information on the listings, as you do with the scholarship books. If you get duplicates, use the application information from the most recently updated online scholarship listing.

Many high schools, colleges, and libraries have purchased scholarship databases with which you can broaden your search. And here's a list of websites that may help in your research:

- Reference Service Press Funding:
  www.rspfunding.com
- FastWeb—Scholarship Search:
  www.fastweb.com
- Scholarships.com:
  www.scholarships.com
- Sallie Mae College Answer:
  www.collegeanswer.com

- U.S. Department of Education:
  www.ed.gov/students
- U.S. Department of Education—
  Federal Student Aid:
  www.studentaid.ed.gov
- National Association of Student Financial
  Aid Administrators (NASFAA):
  www.nasfaa.org

Scholarship Scams

Most scholarships offered to budding college students are on the up-and-up, but some are created for the sole purpose of separating you from your money. Some of the signs of scholarship scams include:

- "We guarantee you'll get a scholarship." In reality, almost every financial aid applicant is eligible for something. A guarantee like this is, therefore, worth nothing.
- "You can't get this information anywhere else." Nonsense. We live in an information-rich society. Any legitimate source of financial aid will make information widely available through a number of means and media. Don't pay a premium for what is free or readily available in an inexpensive format.
- "Credit card or bank account number required to hold scholarship." Don't even think about it. Legitimate scholarship providers do not require this information as a condition for receiving funds.
- "We'll do all the work." OK, this one is tempting. We are all very busy people with a million things to do who feel that we can't possibly find the time to do this kind of research. But there is only one person who is going to benefit from the kind of work that this entails,

and that is you. A pitch like this appeals to the lazy instincts in all of us, but there is no one you can expect to be more motivated to do the research than yourself.

- "The scholarship will cost you some money." This one hardly deserves comment. There is a strong preconception in this country that, as a general rule, you need to spend money to make money. While this may be true on Wall Street, it doesn't apply here. The investment you are making is in your education, and the best resource you can invest is your time.

- "You are a finalist" or "You have been selected" for a scholarship you never applied to. The absurdity of this is clear once you think about it. It is very flattering to think that some organization pored through the records of every person in the country to find that you are the most qualified to receive its generous award—and you didn't even apply! Remember, if it seems too good to be true, it is.

But do take note that just because a scholarship sounds weird or offbeat doesn't mean it's a scam. For instance, the legitimate Stuck-at-Prom scholarship contest rewards high school students who wear duct tape to their prom!

The moral of the story? Do your research. Check out the program before you apply for the cash. Talk to your guidance counselor and your parents, too. They can help you figure it all out.

Application Tips

There are a number of steps involved in applying for scholarships. Here are some tips so you can keep everything on track.

Writing for Applications

Some scholarship providers may have you do initial processing online through a scholarship database, but for many, you are going to have to write to the organization in order to get an application.

- ✓ Use a very simple letter of introduction.
  Use a regular business letter format, and keep it simple so the request moves quickly (see sample letter on page 26). The actual committee that will choose the scholarship recipient probably will not read it, so there is no need to go into great detail about yourself or why you are applying.

- ✓ Try to address the letter to a specific individual.
  If you have a phone number, call to make sure the letter is going directly to the right office. If there is no phone number or specific office, send your letter to the attention of the scholarship's name. Someone in the organization will know which office should receive your request.

- ✓ Mention the specific scholarship you are applying for.
  Some agencies administer more than one! If you ARE applying for more than one of them, use a separate letter for each scholarship, and mail these letters in separate envelopes. Also, if you want the application for only one of that organization's scholarships, you might as well ask them to send

you applications for any other ones that may be appropriate for you. Wouldn't hurt, right?

✓ Mention how you found out about the scholarship.
Many agencies like to know how their information is disseminated. They want to make sure it is going to the correct "market" and to a diverse population. They will appreciate this data as they plan future cycles.

✓ State when you intend to use the money.
That way, they will send you information for the right year.

✓ Include a phone number and/or an email address
Otherwise, the organization can't contact you if they have any questions or need to follow up with you for any reason.

✓ Be sure to date your letter so you remember when it was sent.
You will need to keep track of when you sent letters out. Otherwise, you won't be able to follow up with the organizations who haven't sent you applications in a timely way.

✓ Include a self-addressed, stamped envelope with the letter.
Many of these organizations are nonprofit and will appreciate the help to reduce postage costs. A self-addressed envelope will also get you an earlier response, since the organization won't have to type an envelope. There is no need to send the letter by certified mail.

Here's a sample letter of introduction to get
you started!

```
Today's Date
XYZ Foundation
888 7th Avenue
New York, NY 10101


Attn: Talent Scholarship Office

Dear XYZ Foundation,

I am a high school student at ABC
High School and am applying to
attend John Doe College for next
fall. I would like to receive
application forms for the Talent
Scholarship that I read about in
Kaplan Scholarships.

Also, I would like to receive any
other scholarship or fellowship
program information that is
available through your organization.
Enclosed is a self-addressed,
stamped envelope for your
convenience. I have also provided
a phone number and email address if
you would like to contact me.

Thank you in advance for your
assistance and information.

Sincerely,
Joe Student
100 Main Street
Philadelphia, PA 19100
(555)444-4444
Joe@email.com
```

Increasingly, even small non-profits have webpages. Before writing a letter, make certain that an electronic application is not already available on their site. They may also have an email listed to contact them regarding the scholarships.

Follow-Up Letters

If you still have not received anything after six to eight weeks, it is appropriate to send a second letter. Don't send a different letter that says something about the organization's not getting or answering your first request. At best, you'll come off as pushy. At worst, you'll seem unprofessional or impolite. Just send your original letter (with a new date) again as if it had never been sent to the organization.

If you send a second letter and still receive no response, you might want to call to see if they have the application ready for you and will mail it soon, or if they are no longer offering the scholarship. If you don't have a contact number, use directory assistance. When you do call, remember to be very polite, and begin your conversation by asking general questions about the scholarship. This way you can discreetly find out if it is still being offered.

If it isn't being offered, ask if the organization has any new scholarship programs for which you qualify. If so, ask them to send you an application. If the scholarship is still being offered, tell them you have sent a request and want to make sure they have received it (remember, don't be too aggressive). You may find that it is not easy to confirm that they have the request. If this is the case, ask if you can fax a copy of the letter. Some agencies will be able to tell you if they have the letter, in which case you should ask when you can expect to receive the application.

Be sure to confirm the deadline for submission. Record notes and conversations on the file copy of the letter so you can easily check the status of the search.

And remember, if any organization drops out along the way, you can also apply next year!

The Application

Once you have secured the applications, it's time to begin the process of completing them. You should approach this step as if you are applying for a job. Initial impressions on paper are very important, so you want your application to stand out from all the others.

Be sure to read the entire application and any accompanying instructions before completing it, because failing to answer as instructed might eliminate you from consideration. Type your application and make several photocopies so you can go through some drafts before the final edition. The application should be your own, but seeking input from others can improve it.

Many applications may require supplemental information from other sources. If such information is needed, be sure to plan your time to secure what is requested. Some items, such as academic transcripts and letters of reference, may take some time to obtain. Don't wait until the last minute! You might need recommendations for many of the applications. If this is the case, it is best to have these recommendations tailored to the specific application, because general recommendations do not make as much of an impact.

Find out if the recommendations should be sealed and included with the application or are to be sent in, signed with a signature, separately by the recommendation writers. If the recommendations must be separate, tell the writers not to send them until the day you expect your application to reach the organization, as it is easier for the scholarship provider to match up documents if the application arrives first.

If the instructions say nothing about enclosing other documents, you might consider including a cover letter with your application. It helps differentiate your application from the others, but don't overdo it. A quick summary is all that is needed, highlighting the reasons why you would make an excellent recipient of the scholarship. A letter with bullet points might be most effective.

Remember to Thank Those Who Have Helped You

Remember, the most that many of these organizations and individuals receive in return for their generosity is the occasional thank-you (and maybe a tax deduction!). An expression of gratitude will confirm that they have made the right choice and will lay the groundwork for possible renewals.

Renewing Scholarships for Subsequent Years

Renewal procedures vary depending on the kind of award you receive. Scholarship programs usually require new applications each year from all interested parties. Use the research you have already done to reapply for aid for which you may not have been eligible the previous year.

Once you are in school, there are usually many announcements of large-scale scholarship competitions. Most schools have specific offices that coordinate these prestigious awards. Begin at the aid office; if they don't coordinate or know about these awards, check with the academic dean. Academic deans administer applications for the many awards that are associated with strong academic performance.

Scholarship To-Dos

Grades 9 and 10

✓ Narrow it down.

Looking through information on thousands of scholarships and narrowing down a list to the handful of scholarships that are relevant directly to you is going to be half the battle. That's why you should start as early as possible, so you're not rushing later on.

If you know what career you want to pursue, then you can look for scholarships based on that particular field. But don't stop there! Think about all your academic and extracurricular activities, and look to your strengths! You might be able to find a scholarship that will award you money based on something other than the fact that you want to be an astrophysicist. Of course, if you don't know what you want to study in college, don't worry! There are so many different kinds of scholarships out there; you are bound to find a few that are a great match for you. If you're stumped, you can always ask your guidance counselor for advice on how to move forward with your search.

Remember, you may need to adapt your list as your high school career moves forward. For example, once you know what schools you are definitely applying to, you'll want to find out what scholarships they offer.

✓ Write for applications.
It will take some time for you to get all your letters ready and in the mail. And then it could take weeks for the organization to receive and review your letter. Not to mention the time it'll take for you to actually receive the application. Rather than find yourself in a time crunch, take care of this important step as soon as possible.

Once the initial letters have been mailed, you must carefully keep track of responses. Be sure to note the application deadline (if known) of each scholarship for your records so you can ensure timely submissions.

✓ Create a timetable for applications.
*After you've done all the research and sent
out your letters, you're going to want to
make sure you don't let those application
deadlines slip past you! The best thing to do
is to sit down with a calendar and make a
plan. Below is a summary timeline to help
you out. Grab a calendar and use this general
timeline to help you create your timetable.
This will help you to have all your scholarship
deadlines and to-dos in one place:*

- Two to three years before graduation:
  Do your research, and have the list of your
  scholarships ready.
- One to two years before graduation. Write for
  applications; follow up when necessary until
  you have all the applications you need.
- One year to nine months before graduation:
  Mail all applications with required
  documentation.
- Nine to six months before graduation: Follow
  up with any organization you have not heard a
  decision from (if deadline has passed).
- Summer before college: Notify the financial
  aid office of any scholarships you have been
  awarded. Be sure to ask what effect this will
  have on earlier awards and your options.
- Right before school starts: Write thank-you
  notes to organizations.
- First semester in college: Start getting your
  applications ready for scholarship renewal!

Grades 11 and 12

✓ Review your list and adjust as necessary.
*As mentioned before, the schools you are
definitely applying to might have scholarships
of their own, so be sure to find out about all
scholarships available, what must be done*

to be considered, and—very important—the deadline by which to apply. Much of this information may be at the school's website, specifically on the home page of their financial aid department. (FYI: At some schools, the financial aid officers are more familiar with scholarship sources than the admissions officers.)

✓ Keep to your timetable!
There's no point in doing all that research if you're going to let important dates fly by. Make sure you are keeping on top of your applications and deadlines.

✓ Make sure you've got money for all four years of college.
The college experience lasts more than one year, but many scholarships do not. You'll have to renew them. Therefore, your scholarship research should extend for the number of years you need to complete your degree. In fact, you will need to begin the process for renewing scholarships and finding new sources of aid in your first semester of college! Bottom line: Don't throw away your scholarship list and timetable. You'll need to keep track of all this throughout your college education.

A Note on Social Networking Sites

Be smart about how you use social networking sites. If used carefully and wisely, they can be a tool to help you get into the college or program of your choice.

You can use Facebook for more than just procrastinating; you can use it to network with other students in your school, get information about school groups and clubs, set up study groups, learn more about scholarship or internship programs, and research colleges.

Colleges and universities are beginning to recognize the impact of social networking in the admissions process—with more and more schools putting social networking policies in place. Some admissions officers invite applicants to send them friend requests. Special Facebook accounts are set up in order to interact with applicants or for applicants to ask questions and interact with each other.

Summer, Summer, Summertime

The Summer before Grade 9

Going from middle school to high school can be one of the most difficult transitions in a student's life. Here are some tips for how to get ready!

✓ Talk to your parents about summer tutoring.
  Is there any subject area that you find more challenging than others? The summer could be your chance to catch up before entering high school in the fall.

✓ Do some independent studying.
  Find some workbooks that will keep your mind sharp during the dog days of summer!

✓ Get involved in your community.
  Volunteer at your local community center, or find out how you can help out at your church, temple, or synagogue.

✓ Develop your interests.
  Summer is a good time for personal exploration. Take some time to think about your future and what you want to do.

✓ Take trips with your family.
*Travel is a way to enrich your own knowledge
and expand your experiences while having
fun at the same time. Try visiting at least
one place that you've never been to before.
Day trips can offer just as much value as
extended vacations to faraway places.*

✓ Read!
*Contact your high school to find out if any
books are recommended (or required) for
the summer. Reading serves to increase
your vocabulary, but make sure you approach it as an enjoyable and pleasurable
exercise rather than a chore, because you'll
get more out of it.*

✓ Keep up with your current extracurricular
activities.
*If you've been a member of the Girl Scouts
since the first grade, start planning your Gold
Award. If you play an instrument, continue
lessons or join a local musical group. During
school, your classes may all be academic,
but the summer is a good time to explore
your creative or artistic side.*

✓ Stay physically active.
*Good habits start early in life. Exercise every
day, whether you play basketball with friends
or ride your bicycle to the park, or get up off
the couch with your Nintendo Wii!*

✓ Find a summer program that fits your interests.
*Most local colleges sponsor programs for
elementary and middle school students.
Cultural institutions such as museums, zoos,
theaters, and botanical gardens also have
summer offerings that range from day camps
to weekly classes.*

Chapter 2:
Grade 9

Even if you're not ready to pick a college yet, you can enter into your first year of high school with an awareness of where you'll be going next. This year, you don't have to take admissions tests, look at colleges, or apply for financial aid yet. It's the perfect time, though, to start taking the first steps on the path that will take you to your dream school.

This year, challenge yourself in school: select classes that will stretch your knowledge and skills—and impress colleges down the road. This is a great time to map out the classes you'll take over the next few years; there's always room to make changes, but it will help you to have an idea of where you're heading

Keep in mind that extracurricular activities are important; sign up for things you already love—whatever that means—but also branch out, and be willing to try something that's new to you: maybe volunteering, a new sport, or a club.

Even though you aren't ready to apply for financial aid, it's never too early to get a sense of what's out there. Take some time this year to do your homework where financial aid is concerned: learn what scholarships exist, which ones you might qualify for, and how to be smart when you select and apply for financial aid.

This section will give you tips on easing into high school, maximizing your experiences this year, and having an awesome time in the process.

Quotes from Students Who've Been There, Done That

"At first, I was unhappy with my school. It seemed like everyone was too serious, and the classes were really hard. I was lucky to find a teacher who looked out for me and helped me see that kids at my school are serious about school, but are still fun and interesting."

—Clare, 12th grade

"I knew almost right away that my high school wasn't right for me. Classes were too big and I didn't have the kind of choices I wanted. I am really glad that I listened to my instincts and switched to a smaller school."

—Jesse, 12th grade

"It sounds crazy, but I started looking at colleges in ninth grade and I am so glad I did! I wasn't seriously looking, but it was way less stressful when the time came to narrow down my choices."

—Grace, college freshman

"Don't work too hard to fit in. Just focus on being yourself and doing what you like to do. It might take some time, but you will make great friends who have the same kinds of interests."

—Sierra, 11th grade

"My school required us to meet with the guidance counselor at the beginning of freshman year to plan out our classes for all four years. I changed my plan as the year went along, but it was nice to have it all written down in one place so I knew what to expect."

—Madison, 11th grade

"I hardly knew anyone at my high school and it was really hard to make new friends. Joining the track team gave me a way to be part of a group and get to know more people."

—Lucille, college sophomore

"Take some time to relax and enjoy yourself and meet people. Sure you should be planning and thinking ahead, but for me, the real work of ninth grade was just getting used to being in high school."

—Jessica, 12th grade

"Ninth grade is a good time to do some sampling and learn what subjects, teachers, and activities you like best."

—Grace, college freshman

"Don't be too hard on yourself, but do be aware of your grades, and try to keep them up. It makes things a lot easier later on."

—Ahmet, 12th grade

"I wish I had been more willing to ask my parents for help with all the things I suddenly had to juggle. I felt a lot of pressure to do it all myself, but looking back, they totally would have helped me out if they had known how stressed I was."

—Tasha, college sophomore

Grade 9 To-Dos

Although colleges look at many factors during the admissions process, ultimately they are looking for evidence of just two things: whether you will survive in their academic environment and whether you will contribute to their campus life. What you do inside and outside of high school is the evidence!

Your grades, classes, test scores, and teacher recommendations will provide evidence of your academic abilities. Your extracurricular activities (honors, sports, music, clubs, volunteering, work, etc.) and recommendations will provide evidence of your character, commitment, passion, and leadership.

You can use this checklist throughout grade 9 to help you make sure you're off to a great start:

Academics

✓ It's never too soon to start thinking about college!
  As a freshman, you don't have to know exactly where you want to go to college, but you can get a good idea of what type of college you want to attend. It'll help you plan your course load and other important activities during your high school career.

✓ Get to know your guidance counselor.
  Your counselor can help you get where you want to be.

✓ Get the best grades you can.
  Remember this is the first year where your grades will affect your grade point average (GPA) and will be viewed by colleges.

✓ Plan your course load so that you take the right classes.
  Most colleges require the completion of courses in math, science, English, and social studies. Take the most challenging (but appropriate) courses you can.
  Talk with your counselor about maybe taking the SAT Subject Test for courses you recently completed. It's always best to do it when the class is fresh in your mind!

✓ Develop good study skills.
  Trust us, you don't want to wait until the last minute on this one. It's better to have the skills now!

✓ Form relationships with your favorite teachers.
  Not only will they help you throughout your high school career, you'll feel very comfortable asking them to write the recommendations for your college applications!

Extracurriculars

✓ Find extracurricular activities that spark your interest.

   These can be after-school activities that are organized by your school. There are also activities or hobbies that you do outside of school, like dance classes or Tae Kwan Do. The important thing is to do what you enjoy!

✓ Volunteer!

✓ Read, read, read!

✓ Plan special activities for your summer vacation.

✓ Start a "Things to Brag About" file.

   Record honor roll awards, community service, and anything else you do. Way later, when you're filling out college applications, you'll easily be able to distinguish yourself from the rest of the competition! Create an activity résumé listing all of your accomplishments and activities, such as:

   ○ *Volunteer work*

   ○ *Activities (both in- and out-of-school activities)*

   ○ *Athletics*

   ○ *Honors and awards*

   ○ *Employment*

   ○ *Other accomplishments*

Contests and Awards to Sign Up for in Grade 9

In addition to scholarships, loans, and grants, there exist hundreds of contests that you can enter to win money for college—starting as early as the ninth grade! Many require you to write an essay which might make a great basis for a college admissions essay. How to find these potential gold mines?

- Browse for websites, with search strings such as "contests for college" or "high school contests."
- Check out your school library, public library, and bookstores for books on contests and scholarships.
- Visit your school's career center or ask your counselor.
- Call local organizations and businesses to see if they sponsor contests.
- Skim newspapers and bulletin boards.
- Keep a file on contests and their deadlines, updating it each year.

To Get You Started

- *American Legion Oratorical Contest*
- *Ayn Rand Institute Essay Contests*
- *The Chestnut and Cedar NewMedia Publishing Awards*
- *The DuPont Challenge*
- *National History Day Contest*
- *National Peace Essay Contest*
- *Prudential Spirit of Community Awards*
- *Scholastic Art and Writing Awards*
- *ThinkQuest Internet Challenge*

- *Toshiba/NSTA ExploraVision Awards*
- *Voice of Democracy
  National Competition*
- *Young Naturalist Awards*

Time Management

The Time Management Quiz

Sometimes it feels as if you don't have enough time to do it all. Maybe you really DON'T. So take the Time Management Quiz!

How many hours a week do you spend . . .

1. Sleeping? _____ hours

2. Eating? _____ hours

3. Showering/getting dressed? _____ hours

4. Getting from your home to school and from school to home? _____ hours

5. In school? _____ hours

6. Doing extracurricular activities? _____ hours

7. Doing homework and studying? _____ hours

8. Doing chores or running errands? _____ hours

9. Watching TV, going online, hanging out, etc.? _____ hours

10. Other stuff? _____ hours

Add up the number of hours to see how long it takes to do it all: _____ hours

Is your total MORE than 168 hours?

If you said yes, it looks like you need to make some real changes to how you spend your day! You don't have a lot of flexibility in the first five items. Let's face it, you can't sleep less or get out of school earlier. But the last five items are the areas of your day where you have the most control. You need to reprioritize and reorganize that time!

A Daily Planner Is Your Best Friend

High school is a busy time, between classes, friends, extracurricular activities, studying, family responsibilities, college prep, and the rest. It's tough keeping it all together without pulling your hair out.

If you don't already have a daily planner or electronic scheduler, get one! There is no easier way to keep everything in your life in order. Every assignment due date, test, deadline, or appointment will be all in one place! Having all that information at your fingertips will keep you from stretching yourself too thin. It'll show you, at a glance, how, when, and where you are spending your time.

Go back to the time management quiz, and look at the last five items again. In your planner, make an after-school schedule so you can keep track of each day's activities and commitments. Set up time to study, complete homework, and do a little college prep. Remember to schedule in some time to relax and hang out, too.

Sample After-School Schedule	
3:00–4:00	Extracurricular activity
4:00–4:30	Getting home
4:30–6:30	Homework

Sample After-School Schedule *(con't)*	
6:30–7:30	Dinner
7:30–9:00	Scout Meeting or Religious School
9:00–11:00	TV/Reading
11:00	Bedtime!

Keep to Your Plans!

Now that you've got your life organized, you've got it made, right? Well, yes, as long as you keep to the schedule. If your best friend calls to see if you want to go to the mall in five minutes, check your schedule—if you have already scheduled homework for that time, say NO!

If you have trouble sticking to schedules (or love that snooze button), enlist your friends and family to help you keep on track and on time (i.e., ask a friend to call you one hour after you get home from school to check that you are NOT on your Facebook page).

But remember, just because you keep a schedule doesn't mean you have to give up all of your free time. You have weekends, remember? And keeping to a schedule will make your high school experience less overwhelming, so you can spend less time stressing and more time getting closer to your goal—step-by-step.

Social Networking in Grade 9

Keep It PG!

Potential employers for that summer internship you're applying to may look at your Facebook page, Twitter feed, Flicker album, or pretty much anything else that search engine results give them. They may extend or reject an offer based on what they find there. The bottom line: make sure you're not the next Youtube sensation for all the wrong reasons!

Are there any pictures, links, or content on your page that may make someone question your character or judgment? If so, hit delete!

Facebook To-Dos

- Decide with your parents if you really want a Facebook profile. It's definitely not necessary and can be detrimental. Take down any photos of you (or your friends) that will make admissions officers or potential employers think twice.

- Use a professional-looking photo for your profile picture.

- Remove contact information such as your phone number and address.

- Do not subscribe to any groups that show any bigotry or promote illegal activity.

- As a rule of thumb, set your privacy settings as restrictive as possible. Even if you do this, friends of friends may gain access to your postings or pictures, so be aware.

- Monitor your pictures and postings frequently. Be ready to untag any unflattering photos of you.

- In addition to email, you may want a separate Facebook account for professional use only to help you to track, contact, and network with potential employers and college counselors.

Summer, Summer, Summertime

The Summer before Grade 10

Remember that a lot of the activities you did before grade 9 you can keep doing throughout high school. Just don't go to the same places or reread the same books! Switch it up!

✓ Research scholarships!

✓ Keep writing!

If you take summer courses, make sure that you choose challenging classes that require you to work on your writing and critical thinking skills. You're going to need those skills for the writing portion of the SAT/ACT and for your college essay!

✓ Keep reading!

Check out your local library for lists of recent releases as well as the classics. If you really love to read, take the time during the summer to read as many books by your favorite authors as you can. Reading also serves to boost your vocabulary and language comprehension for the SAT. Kaplan produces versions of several classics such as Frankenstein that are designed to increase your vocabulary and reading comprehension. There are also plenty of online resources to point you in the right direction. For example, the American Library Association (ALA) has book lists online (see http://www.ala.org/ yalsa/booklistsawards/booklistsbook).

Stay in touch with the world around you by reading the newspaper every day. Most of the major national newspapers are available to read online, as are an increasing number of local papers. Make reading the newspaper part of your daily routine, along with checking your email. Also stay abreast of the major weekly magazines (such as Newsweek *or* Time*). You can take out a subscription or read them in your local library.*

✓ Keep up with independent study!
Logic games and puzzles are also good ways to begin preparing for the many standardized tests you will face in the next four years.

✓ Keep traveling!
This summer, write in a diary and take photos of your trips! This is a good way to practice your skills for the college application essay; plus, once you're in college, you'll be able to look back fondly on happy memories of times you spent with your family.

Chapter 3:
Grade 10

So you've finally moved up from the bottom of the high school totem pole! Graduation may still seem a long way off, but this is the year to start laying the groundwork for a seamless transition out of high school and into the next stage of your life.

Taking the PSAT, the PLAN, or both will give you some concrete test-taking experience and an idea of what to expect next year when it's time for the real thing.

If you haven't already, start narrowing down your top college choices—and it is worth thinking about the kinds of programs, classes, and environment you'd like to have access to during your college years.

You might also want to think about taking even more diverse courses this year. Have you ever considered being a "foreign exchange student"? Well, that's just an old-school term for someone who does a study abroad program.

Above all, keep those grades up, and don't slack off on your fun extracurriculars! Freshman year is a time for learning and adjustments, but now you really need to focus. From here on out, do your very best to shine, both in and outside the classroom!

Quotes from Students Who've Been There, Done That

"Definitely put some time into preparing for the PSAT. Even though it doesn't end up on your permanent record, it's a good chance to get ready for the tests that matter."

—Matt, 12th grade

"Sophomore year was kind of in-between: things weren't as new as ninth grade, but I didn't have the pressure of applying to colleges yet. It was a good time to join some clubs and branch out a little."

—Grace, college freshman

"I started putting a little money into a savings account, just $50 from each paycheck at my weekend job. It didn't add up to a huge amount, but it helped so much to have a little cushion during my first year of college."

—Lucille, college sophomore

"In tenth grade, you should work hard at keeping your grades up. That way, even if you have a slipup during the next two years when you have a lot of other stuff going on, colleges can see that you have a solid track record."

—Jesse, 12th grade

"I took some time off during the summer, but I also took an extra class that my school had approved at the community college. That way, I could take one less course during junior year."

—Jessica, 12th grade

"I got to the point where I had so much going on that I had to make a big wall calendar with important due dates. I ended up using it all through my junior and senior years, too."

—Jake, college freshman

"Hold on to some of your best papers and projects. You might want them later for a portfolio or a writing sample."

—Ashley, 12th grade

"I took a service trip to volunteer in another city during the spring break of my sophomore year, and it was an awesome experience. I would recommend it to anyone."

—Colin, college freshman

"I didn't take the PLAN very seriously, but colleges totally responded to my scores and started sending me mail right away."

—Lucas, college freshman

"Honestly, my best advice is to practice sleeping enough and keeping up with your homework. It's so easy to wear yourself down, and it only gets more stressful next year, so you have to take care of yourself."

—Leo, 11th grade

"Volunteer whenever you can, even if it is just for a one-day event. That stuff adds up and makes you look really involved and active."

—Matt, 12th grade.

"I wish I had taken more challenging classes earlier, instead of trying to do the really hard ones during senior year, when I was already so busy with school applications."

—Anh, college sophomore

Grade 10 To-Dos

The choices you make this year will affect your future, so you need stay on top of things! Colleges recognize that freshman year may have been challenging with the transition to high school, but by tenth grade they look for stability.

Plan, Plan, Plan

✓ Meet with your guidance counselor in September.

Time to take another look at your course load and to start talking about your college plans. This is the year to map out your college prep plans with your guidance counselor.

You'll also want to talk to your guidance counselor about taking the PSAT in October or the PLAN test (a practice ACT).

Academics

✓ Devise an academic plan for 10th, 11th, and 12th grades.

Make sure it includes all the required college prep classes. Concentrate on taking the most rigorous classes.

✓ Become familiar with the college entrance exams—the ACT and SAT.

✓ Earn the best grades you can!

✓ Develop strong academic skills in reading, vocabulary, math, and problem-solving.

Extracurricular

✓ Continue to develop your outside interests.

Seek leadership roles in your activities. Colleges love to see students' commitment to their activities.

Other Tips

✓ Read, read, read. Increase your vocabulary for the SAT/ACT.

✓ Find time to look at college websites.

✓ Get to know yourself!
Start thinking: "Who am I? Where am I going? What will I be? What are my strengths, weaknesses, skills, talents, interests, attitudes, summer experiences, short-term goals, long-term goals, personality traits? Write down your responses on a "personal inventory sheet" to be used later for writing your college essay.

✓ Keep your "Things to Brag About" file up-to-date.

✓ Take advantage of summer.

Test Taking in Grade 10

You Don't Have to Wait until Junior Year to Take SAT Subject Tests

SAT Subject Tests are designed to assess your achievement on high school subjects such as history, math, science, English, and foreign languages. You KNOW it's best to take ANY exam while the material is fresh in your mind—so why wait until you forget all of your geometry theorems to take the math Subject Test?

For foreign language Subject Tests, though, you'll do better if you complete AT LEAST two years of study before you take one. *¿Comprendes?*

Deciding which tests to take is easy. Make a list of the colleges you're interested in. Then check out their websites, catalogs, or books to find out how many Subject Tests they require and in which subjects.

Not sure where you want to go to college? Take this checklist to your guidance counselor to help you figure out your SAT Subject Test future.

- Biology/EM
- Chemistry
- Chinese with Listening
- French
- French with Listening
- German
- German with Listening
- Italian
- Japanese with Listening
- Korean with Listening
- Latin
- Literature
- Math Level 1
- Math Level 2
- Modern Hebrew
- Physics
- Spanish
- Spanish with Listening
- U.S. History
- World History

PSAT

The PSAT is a preliminary version of the SAT, which serves as an invaluable practice opportunity—and can open the door to National Merit Scholarships and other awards.

How Is the PSAT Structured and Timed?

The PSAT is two hours and ten minutes long. It's divided into the following sections:

Section	Length	Question Types	Number of Questions
Math	Two 25-minute sections	Multiple Choice	28

Section	Length	Question Types	Number of Questions
		Grid-Ins	10
Critical Reading	Two 25-minute sections	Sentence Completion	13
		Reading Comprehension	35
Writing Skills	One 30-minute section	Identifying Sentence Errors	14
		Improving Sentences	20
		Improving Paragraphs	5

How Can I Register For the PSAT?

You can register with your guidance counselor or at any high school in your community.

What's the Range of Possible PSAT Scores?

Each PSAT section has a scaled score from 20–80 points.

When Can I Take the PSAT?

The PSAT/NMSQT is administered on the third Saturday of October and the preceding Wednesday.

You may be asking yourself, why am I reading about the PSAT in grade 10? Don't high school JUNIORS take that test? Well, yes, most people take it in the spring of grade 11, but sophomores can take it, too. And you should consider taking the PSAT in your sophomore year, even though it doesn't count.

We know what you're thinking . . . WHAT? Take a test that doesn't count? Why would you EVER want to take a test that DOESN'T count?!?!?

The reason is because when you take it again in grade 11—when it DOES matter—you'll know what to expect. Not to mention that you'll probably get a better score! They don't call it the SAT's kid brother for nothing. At the very least, you'll get some extra practice for what can be an intimidating exam. And you know that practice makes . . . perfect!

Soon after the test, you will mysteriously begin to receive college catalogs and brochures about special programs, giving you a sneak peek at what's out there.

But remember, you DO have to take it again in grade 11, even if you ace it in sophomore year. The eligibility requirements for some scholarships require it.

A Note on National Merit Scholarships®

The National Merit Scholarship Corporation hands out over $50 million to more than 10,000 college (and college-bound) students. You are automatically registered when you take the PSAT and will be notified if you are eligible to participate in the program based on your PSAT score. Then you must meet eligibility requirements (found at www. nationalmerit.org). Even if you don't score super duper high on the PSAT, there are some National Merit Special Scholarships sponsored by specific companies for their employees children (remember to have your parents ask if these apply to you).

PLAN

If you're thinking of taking the ACT, you may choose to take the PLAN, sort of an ACT practice test, during your sophomore year. PLAN scores aren't reported to colleges, but they can give you a helpful sense of whether you're on track, or need to brush up a little bit, for your college preparation.

The four academic sections of the PLAN test your grasp of high school–level English, reading, science, and math. The report also gives you an estimated ACT score based on how well you performed on the PLAN. Unlike college entrance exams, though, the PLAN also includes assessments of your interests and career prospects—so when you get your score report, you'll receive some information about fields or specific careers that are a good fit based on your responses. These might be as general as "management" or as specific as "animal trainer" or "cheesemaker"!

You can use your PLAN score report to help you focus your studying as you prepare for the ACT. You might also want to show it to a parent or guidance counselor and collaborate on a revised plan for your remaining high school courses. That way, you'll know that you're well prepared for all kinds of academic and career possibilities—not just cheesemaking!

To learn more about how to take the PLAN, see sample questions, or to try out some of the career exploration tools the test uses, visit the official website at *www.act.org/plan/index.html*.

Reading Is a Test Score Booster

Reading helps your score in two ways:

- The more you read, the more you cultivate your comprehension skills.
- Reading builds your vocabulary without you even trying!

If your only reading comes from school assignments, you probably think that books are boring, cumbersome, and uninteresting. But reading doesn't have to be boring to be beneficial! You can get lots of great vocab help from your favorite reading materials, like comic books, teen book series, fashion mags, even celebrity rags! To find new novels that other people are reading, take a look at national best-seller lists—these will give you a good idea of what's widely read. In a given week, novels on the *New York Times* Best-seller List (*www.nytimes. com*) might cover Afghani history, forensic pathology, and small-town mystery. If you can think of a novel you have especially liked, a librarian or bookseller can recommend other titles that might appeal to you.

You can also branch out by reading nonfiction—if it's a subject that interests you, it doesn't have to be dry or boring. Try these on for size:

- *Let Me Play: The Story of Title IX: The Law That Changed the Future of Girls in America*, by Karen Blumenthal
- *Good Brother, Bad Brother: The Story of Edwin Booth and John Wilkes Booth*, by James Cross Giblin
- *True Notebooks: A Writer's Year at Juvenile Hall*, by Mark Salzman

For more suggestions, including audiobooks, DVDs and videos, and graphic novels, visit the American Library Association's Young Adult Library Services Association website at *http://www.ala.org/yalsa/booklistsawards/booklistsbook*.

Set a goal to read for at least 30 minutes every day. You'll be surprised at how easy it is to find the time! If you come across vocabulary you don't know, mark the word and look it up in the dictionary. Keep a list of all of the words you look up in a certain amount of time, like two weeks. Then you can make flash cards containing new words and their definitions for more vocab practice.

You CAN Become a Better Test Taker

Many students complain that they're just not good at taking tests like the SAT or ACT, the very tests that help determine their academic future. But every student can improve his or her test-taking skills. Here's how:

- Do NOT go into a test cold. Familiarize yourself with the exam. That means understanding the format and directions, as well as knowing what kinds of questions will be asked.

- Practice taking exams under testlike conditions. You can find free practice tests at *www.kaptest.com* to get you started!

- Develop strategies for taking standardized tests, such as knowing when to guess or how to back-solve a math equation.

- Run through a practice test again . . . and again . . . and again—especially if you're someone who tends to freeze under pressure. The more you do it, the less nervous you'll be when you take the real thing.

- Go into the test with confidence. A positive attitude goes a long way!

As you can see, the best way to get the confidence you need to ace the tests is to know the test like the back of your hand, learn effective test-taking skills, and practice! Talk to you parents about these tests and how to prepare for them. There are plenty of options out there to give you the guidance and practice you need, like classroom courses, tutoring, and online courses, too! Don't forget about good ol' test prep books out there. They can help you with everything you need to know, like *Kaplan PSAT Premier, Kaplan SAT Premier, Kaplan ACT Premier*, as well as extra stuff like workbooks and flash cards to help you along the way. Whatever you do, don't go into the test center cold turkey!

Seeking Help from Test Prep Professionals

For some, creating your own study schedule for yourself just doesn't cut it. Take the following quiz to see if you need a pro's help.

Do you:

1) Keep saying that you'll study for the SAT tomorrow?
☐ yes ☐ no

2) Have trouble understanding why you're getting questions wrong?
☐ yes ☐ no

3) Jump from topic to topic without focus?
☐ yes ☐ no

4) Find yourself unable to complete a section in the allotted time?
☐ yes ☐ no

If you answered "yes" to any of these questions, you might need a little structure to your study time. A pro can streamline study time and teach you test-taking strategies. Visit *www.kaptest.com* for some potential options based on your needs and budget.

Time and Stress Management

You've got a laundry list of precollege stuff that needs to get done—on top of keeping up with your grades, extra-curricular activities, and everything else high school life has to offer. You're gonna need some help. Here's how to approach it!

Homework Help Websites

Puzzled by a geometry problem? Need to research James Madison? Wonder what a haiku is? When you're stuck, homework help websites abound. However, only you can determine which are most helpful, so browse and discover!

Reading Lists

One of the best exercises for college prep is to read, read, read! Reading encourages analytical skills and primes you for the tons of reading you will be doing in college.

- *www.ala.org/yalsa/booklists*
- *www.freevocabulary.com*

Studying, Problem-Solving, and Time Managements Skills

- *www.collegeboard.com/student/plan/index.html*
- *www.how-to-study.com*

Resources for Homework Assignments

- *www.bjpinchbeck.com*
  B. J. Pinchbeck's renowned Homework Helper has links to over 700 sites of useful information for homework assignments.

- *http://highschoolace.com/ace/ace.cfm*
  High School Ace includes reference sources, college information, and study guides.

- *www.biography.com*
  This site offers a collection of brief sketches covering over 20,000 diverse personalities, including historical and sports figures, politicians, and entertainers.

- *www.nytimes.com/learning*
  At the *New York Times* Learning Network, you can read the day's top news stories, take a quiz, write a letter to the editor, or ask a reporter a question.

- *https://www.khanacademy.org/*
  A library of over 3000 skills ranging from math to history.

Delegating Tasks to Your Parents

Handing over a few small tasks to your parents, if they're interested, keeps them involved, while leaving you more time to take on the rest. You can ask them to do such tasks as:

- Help keep track of application deadlines
- Plan college tours around your schedule
- Investigate financial aid options
- Help you gather information about academic programs at your top-choice colleges
- Proofread essays
- Drive you to college fairs, tours, and to the mall to buy stuff for your dorm room

Much Too Much

If your parents are smothering you with "help," talk to them about it. Explain that you need quiet time to focus on your college decisions and tasks. When you arrive at a decision or complete a task, keep them in the loop by updating them. You will impress Mom and Dad (and yourself) by being able to tackle the admissions process and express yourself clearly.

Networking

It's not only WHAT you know . . . who you know is important, too. If you have questions about college searches and applications, there are plenty of people who can help you! And people are more inclined to lend a hand to those they know and like before they'd aid a stranger. And when it comes to college admissions, students need all the help they can get. So schmooze it up! How do you schmooze? Simple:

- Get out there: Be an active member in your church or other community organization.
- Be friendly: Talk to as many people as possible.
- Be helpful: If you can make someone's life easier, do it. It could be as simple as setting up a phone call between your brother who attends Purdue and the head cheerleader who wants to go there.
- Let them know what your goals are: Whether it's a rewarding summer job, a possible scholarship, or just a date for the prom. You never know who can help.
- Say "thank you": Mom's right—when someone helps you out, make sure to take the time to write a thank-you note. It will be appreciated, and it will encourage that person to support you in the future.
- Return the favor: Like any relationship, it's got to work both ways.

Finding a Mentor

There is so much to be gained from a mentor's help . . . guidance, something to aspire toward, and perspective from an adult who isn't related to you!

Finding a mentor usually comes naturally. It could be your favorite teacher or coach, the owner of a trendy café, your volunteer coordinator, an older and successful student, or a family friend whom you admire. It doesn't really matter WHO it is—just as long as he or she is a positive influence on your life. If you're having trouble finding a mentor, talk to a teacher or guidance counselor about tutoring or mentoring programs in your high school or community.

A great way to break the ice or just connect more and more with your mentor is to take him or her to lunch! As she is picking on a slice of pizza, you can be picking her brain. (Ask her to tell you her life story!) How did she get to be the person she is today? What kind of dreams did she have when she was your age?

Having a role model is informative, fun, and can build your confidence about the choice YOU are making for YOUR life!

More Programs to Consider

The IB Program

The International Baccalaureate (IB) Program is a tough preuniversity curriculum that accepts highly motivated and academically talented high schoolers. Living in a "global village," these kids are challenged to think critically, research deeply, and develop internationally minded perspectives on a broad range of issues.

The IB Program was established in 1968 in Switzerland by a group of teachers who were looking to create a broad curriculum with consistent assessment standards adaptable to any country. The IB Program's goal was to develop caring young people capable of succeeding in university programs around the globe and capable of creating a better and more peaceful world through intercultural understanding and respect. Today, the IB Program includes 3,490 schools in 144 countries. Over 1,000 American high schools offer IB classes.

The diploma program takes two years, so it would take up your junior and senior years. Diploma candidates take comprehensive courses in six subject areas, three at a higher level (this is like an honors or AP class) and three at a standard level. Among other requirements (a thesis-like essay; a special course that explores the nature of knowledge across disciplines; and arts, athletic, and service requirements), you must pass the final exams in your senior year in order to receive the diploma. Exams are taken in May or November.

Sound like your cup of tea? Visit *www.ibo.org.*

Study Abroad Programs

One of the most enriching experiences available to high school students is the study abroad program. The focus of the programs can vary, though most fall into the following categories:

- Language immersion
- Cultural exploration
- Adventure travel
- Community service

Language immersion programs are very popular, and they are an incredibly powerful way to improve your skills in the language you are studying in school. Many students choose a type of program where they spend time with a host family. Others may choose a program where they stay in a boarding facility with a group of students. The advantage of these language immersion programs over traditional language study is the unique, around-the-clock opportunity to improve your speaking and writing skills and your reading and listening comprehension in that language.

You also get a fascinating firsthand, in-depth look at a culture you may not encounter every day, and you get to travel to new places! This, of course, is also the advantage of the cultural exploration and community service programs. The only difference is that the focus is not on improving language skills, but on opening students' minds to new cultures and to important social, economic, and political issues in the world today.

So how do you decide where to go? Talk to your guidance counselor, of course! He or she will have a lot of information on the various programs available, especially those that students from your high school commonly participate in. If you already know what city or country you'd like to explore, great! But you also need to think about cost and safety—two big things that your parents will be most concerned about. Some programs offer scholarships, so don't be discouraged by a potentially high cost. Other issues that may affect your decision include:

- Climate
- Start and end dates of the program
- You have family living in the selected country (or originating there)
- Housing options (host family or dormitory)
- Whether past years' students found the program fun and rewarding
- Ease of application
- Ability to transfer credits

Your guidance counselor can help you work all this out, so you can speak intelligently about these programs with your parents.

You will also need your guidance counselor's help during the application process and to ensure that you can get academic credit for a summer, semester, or year abroad. If you'd like to learn more about study abroad programs, here are some websites you can peruse:

- Council on Standards for International Education Travel: *www.csiet.org*
- Forum on Education Abroad: *www.forumea.org*
- Academic Year in America: High School Foreign Exchange Programs: *http://academicyear.org*
- American Institute for Foreign Study: *http://aifs.com*
- International Studies Abroad: *www.studyabroaddirectory.com*
- Transitions Abroad: *http://transitionsabroad.com*
- Rotary Youth Exchange: http://www.rotary. org/en/StudentsAndYouth/YouthPrograms/ RotaryYouthExchange/Pages/ridefault.aspx

Time to Begin
Your College Search

The Seven Factors for Finding the Right College

When trying to find the right college for you, keep the seven factors for finding the right college in mind:

1) **Academics:** Consider the college's educational value, availability of majors, number and quality of faculty, and its overall reputation.

2) **Location:** Do you want to study in a rural location, where there are fewer distractions but fewer off-campus activities? Or are you into suburban or city life, where there are more internship opportunities but at the cost of expensive housing and higher crime rates?

3) **Climate:** This can also be a factor for many people. If you're thinking about Northwestern, you'd better be prepared for those subarctic Illinois winters! This goes both ways. If you're used to all four seasons, you're going to miss them if you go to the University of Miami in sunny South Florida.

4) **Size:** Pretty self-explanatory—small, medium, or supersized.

5) **Campus life:** Make sure the college supports your lifestyle—academically and socially. After all, you won't be studying 24/7. If you want to play football, make sure your prospective college has a football team!

6) **Special services:** If you are a student with learning or other disabilities, be sure the campus offers the appropriate support.

7) **Cost:** Consider tuition and room and board, of course. Also, a college may require you to pay fees for equipment and labs, health services, parking, and nonresident fees (if you live

out-of-state). Don't forget to budget for text-books and travel expenses (if you go to college far from home).

Research Colleges on the Web

Begin your college search on the right foot. Download valuable information from one of the big college search engines, such as Collegeboard.com or Fastweb.com, where you'll find thousands of statistics, along with college prep, career, and financial aid info.

Once you've sifted through the stats, go to official college websites to learn about majors and requirements, view pictures of the campus, and find out about the faculty, student services, and whatever else you're interested in.

To get a well-rounded view of a college, be sure to check out their online resources on:

- The student newspaper: See what issues concern the student body and what's going on around campus.

- The athletic department: If sports is what you're all about, go to the athletic department's home page to learn about the college's varsity teams and schedules, as well as their intramural programs and fitness facilities.

- The calendar of campus events: If you've got some artistic inclinations, look for the campus arts center's calendar of events to find out what kinds of musical and theatrical events they host or sponsor.

- Recent press releases: You can find this from the campus information department home page. Read about new buildings and programs, student and faculty awards and honors, and achievements in sports, among other newsworthy items.

Now it's time to get the "unofficial" take on your top picks. Log on to the websites below to get a personal perspective on your favorite colleges:

- *www.studentadvisor.com*: A fun site that not only offers you the usual college comparisons but also connects you with behind-the-scenes info about what life on the various campuses is REALLY like.

- *www.collegeconfidential.com*: A great college search engine with cool top-ten lists and more. One highlight is the message board, where you can talk to other students (and parents, too) about the stress of getting into a college, among other things. They also offer college counseling (for a fee) if you need additional help choosing a college.

- *www.studentsreview.com*: Here you'll get— you guessed it—student reviews of colleges, as well as links to related sites.

- *www.teenink.com*: Read college reviews and essays—written BY students FOR students— as well as opinions on a whole lot of other stuff. Don't forget to check out the cool bulletin board, where you can rant and rave about your college search or just jot down your deepest thoughts for all to see.

Remember, don't spend ALL your time surfing the Internet for college information. Talk with your counselor, too!

Create a College Fact Chart

Put all your college facts in one place. Use the following as a model for your chart of college "snapshots"—then you can easily compare and contrast important features and information. This will help you decide which college to choose.

College Name	_____	_____	_____
General Location?	_____	_____	_____
Public/Private?	_____	_____	_____
Religious Affiliation?	_____	_____	_____
Number of Undergrads?	_____	_____	_____
Freshman Retention Rate?	_____	_____	_____
Academics?	_____	_____	_____
Tough/Manageable/Easy?	_____	_____	_____
Workload?	_____	_____	_____
Class Size?	_____	_____	_____
Majors of Interest?	_____	_____	_____
Student Body?	_____	_____	_____
Appearance/Style?	_____	_____	_____
Friendly?	_____	_____	_____
Enthusiastic?	_____	_____	_____
Diverse?	_____	_____	_____
Campus Facilities?	_____	_____	_____
Dorms?	_____	_____	_____
Library?	_____	_____	_____
Internet?	_____	_____	_____
Student Center?	_____	_____	_____
Athletic Complex?	_____	_____	_____

Social Life?	_____	_____	_____
Fraternities/ Sororities?	_____	_____	_____
Active Campus Life?	_____	_____	_____
Off-Campus Activities?	_____	_____	_____
Overall Impression	_____	_____	_____

Should You Apply to Selective Colleges?

These days, most students apply to a minimum of six colleges. You might want to pick two that are dream choices, two that are realistic, and two that are "safety" choices. Seek out colleges that best match your interests, grades, and test scores. Most college websites will provide a profile of their average applicant; visit search programs such as Collegeboard.com or Fastweb.com.

What if you feel you will be more successful—have better grades, higher class rank, more self-confidence—at a less selective school? That's something to consider. It may surprise you to learn that the National Bureau of Economic Research found "students who attend more selective colleges do not earn more than other students who were accepted and rejected by comparable schools but attended less selective colleges." To check out school selectivity by state, browse *www.scholarstuff.com.*

The Most Selective Schools

As you know, selective colleges do not admit everyone who applies, and not all who are accepted attend those schools.

School	Number Applied	% Accepted	% Accepted Who Attended
Juilliard School	2,314	6.7%	70.1%
Yale University	28,975	6.80	70.0
Harvard University	34,302	5.90	79.3
Princeton University	26,664	7.86	68.6
Stanford University	36,632	6.60	67.7
Columbia University	31,818	7.40	58.2
MIT	18,109	8.90	66.2
Cal Tech	3,332	17.2	37.7
Pomona College	5,439	17.5	39.7
Univ. of Pennsylvania	20,483	17.7	66.2
Amherst College	6,142	18.6	37.9
Georgetown University	16,171	20.0	48.9

Your Parents' College Expectations versus Yours

Parents mean well—they really do. But sometimes they can be a real drag when it comes to "helping you" choose a college, especially if they're trying to convince you to go to their alma mater.

Talk to your parents about your college expectations—and theirs—before you begin your search so everyone is on the same page. You don't want to find out that your parents have opinions that dramatically differ from yours months into your search! The two most important factors to discuss are:

1) **Cost:** You want to know if your parents can afford tuition and, if so, how much. This information will affect your college search parameters. Don't, however, give up on a college based on its price tag—find out specifics about financial aid first!

2) **Distance from home:** Find out how your parents feel about the location of the schools you are applying to (and eventually, your ultimate choice). If you decide to stay close to home, discuss your preferences to either commute from home or to live in a dorm on campus, then ask your parents what they think. Remember, there are housing and meal plan fees that you and your parents will have to consider if you want to live on campus. In fact, most college students do commute from home and have a great time!

Discuss any disagreements, and try to come to an agreement on your college options—communication is key to compromise. Here are some more tips on how to get around common situations:

- Do the research on your favorites AND theirs. If you totally rule out their alma maters, do it because you found out that they're really not right for you, not just because you want to be different from Mom or Dad.

- Speak intelligently about the colleges that interest you. Show your parents that you're taking college seriously and that you have tangible reasons for liking your top picks.

- Be assertive, NOT emotional. If you don't want to attend your parents' old colleges, tell them (nicely). It's not OK to blow up at them—even if they're really pressuring you—because a) they're your parents (duh), b) it will make you seem immature and ruin your clever argument, and c) they might be paying your bills.

Questions to Ask Your Guidance Counselor

You're going to have a lot of questions about selecting colleges to apply to. Don't forget that you have your guidance counselor's expertise at your beck and call! Here are the points you should definitely discuss with your guidance counselor:

- "By what date should I give you the list of colleges I'd like to apply to?"
- "These are the colleges I'm considering—do you think they are good matches for me?"
- "Are there any other colleges you would recommend?"

Create a Professional Email Address

Do you really want to send applications to college admissions officers—the very people you are trying to impress—from your *"uknowuwantme@gmail.com"* or *"sugarlips@2cute.com"* email address? Didn't think so.

Drop this book right now and register for a new-and-improved email address with a formal ID. Check out Yahoo, MSN, and Gmail for free email accounts. Once it's all set up, use this email address specifically for anything related to your college search—for college fairs, at admissions and scholarship websites, everything! That way, you can keep all of your correspondence with admissions departments and references organized.

When you create your new account, use your name or initials. If you can't use your name alone because it's already been used, try including your middle initial somehow or the year of your graduation, like *Your.I.Name@yahoo.com*, *YIN2012@gmail.com*, or *Your.Name2014@yahoo.com*.

College Search To-Dos

✓ Talk to your parents about their expectations
  . . . and yours!
  *Make sure you are all on the same page
  about the important issues, especially cost
  (or how tuition is going to be paid) and the
  distance from home.*

✓ Do your research.
  *Start with the big college search engines or
  buy a college guide from your local bookstore. Don't forget to get the "unofficial"
  take on the colleges you like.*

✓ Keep a college fact chart.
  It'll help you keep all the facts organized!

✓ Talk to your guidance counselor.
  *Once you've got an idea about where you
  want to apply, talk to your guidance counselor about your choices. He or she can give
  you lots of ideas and insights!*

Social Networking in Grade 10

Self-Promote

Social networking sites can leave a bad impression, but
they can also make a good impression if you use them
to your advantage. Sites like Facebook are great free
self-promoting tools. Make yourself look good to potential employers, teachers, or college counselors.

It's never too early to gain exposure so that people know about your interests, talents, and abilities. If you've published poems, sold artwork, built a house, cleaned up graffiti, or volunteered for a local homeless shelter, you may want to post videos, photos, or blog entries about your experience. It may help distinguish you from other candidates.

Recording your experiences will also help you later on as you write your college application essays. If you went on an extensive trek through the desert over the summer, posting pictures and writing about your experiences in a photo blog, for example, will help you to relate and keep track of your accomplishments.

Just think twice before posting anything. If it's private, keep it private!

Facebook To-Dos

- Post pictures of yourself doing positive things, such as: working as a volunteer, winning an award, singing in your church choir, or scoring a soccer goal.

- Promote your achievements. If you are a member of the National Honor Society, join their Facebook page! It will help make you more visible to any college admissions counselor who might be interested in looking at your profile.

- Promote your interests. Post links on your profile to websites that you have created or maintain. Link to blogs you follow or organizations you contribute to.

- Post your travel pictures. This shows you're a worldly, well-rounded person.

- Join groups that have positive messages, like cancer awareness or youth empowerment causes.

Summer, Summer, Summertime

The Summer before Grade 11

✓ Find an internship.

An internship can give you insight into different careers and help to focus your own interests. If you already have an idea of what you want to do, an internship will give you valuable work experience that can often lead to a paid position during the summer while you're in college. After you graduate from college, it's usually easier to find jobs in your chosen field if you have some internships under your belt. Start early! Most internships are given to juniors or seniors.

✓ Earn some money.

You can demonstrate your own commitment and responsibility by finding a job and sticking to it. Admissions counselors look for leadership qualities in prospective students. A job can demonstrate these qualities if you can show some sort of progress over time.

✓ Seek out opportunities for community service.

When applying for college, you want to be able to fill in every single line of the section on extracurricular and volunteer activities. In addition, your chances for many scholarships depend on being able to demonstrate that you have a passion for helping others.

✓ Visit a museum.

Major museums often provide special cards for high school students to get in for free. Call each museum's education department for more information. Many museums also offer free classes during the summer as well as during the school year.

✓ Look into summer programs that are part of initiatives such as Outward Bound or GEAR UP.

These programs are designed to help disad-vantaged students prepare for college. Ask your guidance counselor if your school has any affiliations with these and other TRIO programs, or search online. While these pro-grams are often geared more toward tutoring and other kinds of academic preparation, they are often on the cutting edge of hands-on learning.

✓ Keep reading, writing, and traveling!

Chapter 4:
Grade 11

This year, you may begin to feel like the pressure's on—but hopefully, you have already been building a great foundation that will help you get through the year with a minimum of stress.

College fairs and other events are a good opportunity to research schools, meet admissions staff, and learn more about the opportunities you have. Plan on visiting as many schools as you're able to—there is really no substitute for experiencing a campus firsthand. If your schools are local, you'll have a lot more flexibility in planning your visit. Your high school may even take a field trip to colleges in the area. If you're going to be doing some traveling, think ahead: your spring break is a great time to set aside for this, or you and your family can plan another time to go.

You'll also be taking the SAT, the ACT, or both this year. They are high-stakes tests, but with the right kind of preparation, you can approach test day—and the rest of the college application process—feeling relaxed and confident. Read on to find out how.

Grade 11 To-Dos

Eleventh grade is a big year for college planning! From taking your standardized tests to starting the college selection process—you've got a lot to do to stay on top of things! And, of course, this year is superimportant when it comes to grades. If you stay focused and follow our guidelines, you shouldn't get overwhelmed.

Plan, Plan, Plan

✓ Meet with your high school guidance counselor in September!
   Time to review your courses, credit, senior classes, and test dates. Plan to take strong

academic classes during your senior year, rather than load up on electives!

✓ Register for the October PSAT/NMSQT test. *This test will help you figure out your strengths and weaknesses so that you can better prepare for the SAT. Also, the top scorers become eligible for scholarships. Some companies even offer scholarships to employees' children, so make sure your parents ask about this at work.*

✓ Take the ACT and/or SAT test in the spring. *Whichever tests you plan on taking, make sure you're ready. Start prepping now! There are loads of test prep options: books with practice tests, online courses, in-person classes, and private tutors!*

Academics

✓ Strive to achieve your academic best. *Colleges consider junior year very important!*

Extracurricular

✓ Stay involved. *Deep, consistent involvement in school and community activities is a must! Colleges look to see how you spend your time outside of the classroom. Try for a leadership role.*

Other Tips

✓ Start a file to keep college catalogs and brochures organized. *This year you are going to be attending college nights, college fairs, and meeting with college admissions reps at your high school.*

✓ Think and plan SERIOUSLY for financial aid opportunities.

This is the time to really kick your financial aid plans into high gear, especially if you are applying for scholarships. Having the BEST application in the whole wide world won't count for bupkus if you seriously slack off on your financial aid to-dos.

✓ Campus visit time!
Visit schools you may be considering. If this is not practical for you, do visit nearby colleges to get an idea of the different types of schools. Or go online! Some schools have virtual tours available.

✓ Fill out the NCAA forms!
If you plan to play sports at the college level, be sure to fill out NCAA forms in August (before senior year).

✓ College recommendations.
Start thinking about who you'll ask. Then ask if they would write one for you. Many teachers and counselors like to write their recommendations over the summer.

✓ Take advantage of summer.
Do something interesting! Summer is also the perfect time to start brainstorming for your college essay topic. (Remember that personal brag list you've got going? Since your essay should be a reflection of your personality and interests, take a look at that sheet.)

Test Taking in Grade 11

SAT and ACT

Admissions officers use SAT and ACT scores to gauge your academic potential in college. They are standardized paper-and-pencil tests that measure your critical thinking skills—in other words, your ability to analyze and solve problems in math, critical reading, and writing.

Who Should Take the SAT and ACT?

You! The test is always a requirement for the stellar college applications you'll be writing next year! Most high school students take these tests for the first time in the spring of their junior year. This gives them enough time to retake the test during the fall of their senior year if they aren't satisfied with their score.

How Is the SAT Structured and Timed?

The SAT is three hours and 45 minutes long and is divided into the following sections:

Section	Length	Question Types	Number of Questions
Critical Reading	Two 25-minute sections	Sentence Completion	19
	One 20-minute section	Reading Comprehension	48
Math	Two 25-minute sections	Multiple Choice	44
	One 10-minute section	Grid-Ins	10
Writing	One 25-minute section	Identifying Sentence Errors	18
	One 10-minute section	Improving Sentences	25
		Improving Paragraphs	6
	One 25-minute essay	Essay	
Experimental	One 25-minute section	It can be a Critical Reading, Math, or Writing section. Does not count toward score.	Varies

How Will the Test Sections Be Ordered?

The 25-minute essay will always be the first section of the SAT, and the 10-minute multiple-choice writing section will always be last. The other eight sections (including the unscored, experimental section) can appear in any order.

How Can I Register for the SAT, and How Much Does It Cost?

The cost is $50. You can register online at www.collegeboard.org.

What Is the Range of Possible SAT Scores?

Each section is scored from 200–800 each, giving a total range of 600–2,400 points. The essay is scored from 0–12, which is included as one-fourth of the total Writing score.

How Is the ACT Structured and Timed?

The ACT lasts two hours and 55 minutes (excluding the Writing Test) or three hours and 25 minutes (including the Writing Test):

Section	Length	Question Types	Number of Questions
English Test	45 minutes	Usage/Mechanics	40
		Rhetorical Skills	35
Mathematics Test	60 minutes	Arithmetic	14
		Elementary Algebra	10
		Intermediate Algebra	9
		Coordinate Geometry	9
		Plane Geometry	14

Section	Length	Question Types	Number of Questions
Math Test Cont.		Trigonometry	4
Reading Test	35 minutes	Social Studies	10
		Natural Sciences	10
		Prose Fiction	10
		Humanities	10
Science Test	35 minutes	Data Representation	15
		Research Summary	18
		Conflicting Viewpoint	7
Writing Test	30 minutes		1
	You are asked to respond (Optional Essay) to a question about your position on the issue described in the writing prompt.		

How Can I Register for the ACT, and How Much Does It Cost?

You can register online at *www.actstudent.org*.

- Test fee: $35, includes having your scores sent to four colleges.
- Test fee (with the Writing Test): $50.50, includes having your scores sent to four colleges.

What Is the Range of Possible Act Scores?

Each of the four multiple-choice ACT test sections (English, mathematics, reading, and science) is scored on a scale of 1–36. You will also receive a composite score, which is the average of your four test scores (1–36).

If you take the Writing Test, you will receive a Writing Test subscore (ranging from 0 to 12) and a combined English/Writing score (ranging from 1 to 36), along with comments about your essay. Keep in mind that you must take both the English and Writing Tests to receive Writing scores. The Combined English/Writing score is created by using a formula that weighs the English Test score as two-thirds and the Writing Test score as one-third to form a combined score. This combined score is then reported on a 1–36 scale. Please note that taking the Writing Test does not affect your subject area scores or your composite score.

Which Tests Should I Take?

What tests you take will, of course, be decided by the schools you apply to. Almost all competitive schools accept both SAT and ACT scores, but you should be sure to confirm this.

If all of the schools you plan to apply to accept both tests, then the question becomes even more pertinent because essentially, you could take just one. So how do you choose? The SAT is two-thirds critical reading and writing and one-third math. The ACT is one-half English and reading and one-half math and science. So if you're strong in English, you might want to take the SAT. If you're awesome in math and science, but not so good in English, you might do better on the ACT.

For the most up-to-date information and resources on these exams, including timelines for when to take tests and test prep options, visit *www.kaptest.com*.

Taking the SAT and ACT More Than Once

You can take the SAT or ACT more than once—in fact, you probably should!

Take the test for the first time in the spring of junior year. If you don't do as well as you'd like, then take it again in fall of senior year.

Chances are you will perform BETTER the second time around. Why?

- You already did it once, so you won't be as nervous.
- You identified your weaknesses and had time to strengthen them.
- You know the ins and outs of the test, as well as the strategies you need to ace it.
- You will have completed more course work and read more.

Who should retake the exam?

- Students who received low scores
- Students who just missed making the numbers required by their colleges of choice
- Students who froze during the test and know they can do better

It's true that SOME schools combine your two scores if you retake the test, but 80 percent of schools evaluate only your top number. So in the unlikely event you perform worse the second time around, it probably won't matter.

Test Day Tips: Quotes from Students Who've Been There, Done That

"Start looking through prep books early, even if it's just getting a look at the questions and ideas. My experience was that the longer you've been exposed to the concepts, the better grasp you'll have of them."
—Frances, 11th grade

"Know the format of the test you're taking—if you've seen the types of questions for a test a million times, you don't have to waste time trying to figure out what they're asking you to do and how you'll approach them."
—Jesse, 12th grade

"The night before the test, do something fun and relaxing. At that point, cramming isn't going to make a difference, so you might as well enjoy yourself and calm your nerves."

—Clare, 12th grade

"I can't overstate how much it helps to understand what the test will look like, what kinds of topics it covers, and that kind of stuff. Knowing your enemy is the biggest part of the battle!"

—Lucille, college sophomore

"I studied really hard for the SAT, even though a lot of my friends blew it off, and I was glad that I did. Afterward, I was relaxed while I waited for my scores. I felt like, well, I already did my best."

—Colin, college freshman

Test Taking To-Dos

✓ Study, study, STUDY!
Create a study plan, buy some books, take a class. Do whatever you have to do, but be prepared!

✓ Make sure you register!
Wouldn't it be awful if you spent mad time studying and preparing, and then forgot to register! Sure, there's always senior year . . . but it would be so much better if you could use that test as a backup, not your be-all and end-all test date.

✓ A week before the test:
Know exactly where you're going, exactly how you're getting there, and exactly how long it takes to get there. It's probably a good idea to visit your test center sometime before the day of the test so that you know what to expect—what the rooms are like, how the desks are set up, and so on.

✓ Three days before the test:
Take a full-length practice test under timed

conditions. Approach the test strategically, actively, and confidently.

We don't recommend taking a full practice SAT or ACT if you have fewer than 48 hours left before the test. Doing so will probably exhaust you and hurt your score on the actual test. Remember, the SAT and ACT are marathons, and you are a runner. Runners don't run a marathon the day before the real thing.

✓ The day before the test:
Just as we don't suggest you take a practice test right before the real one, we also think that studying the day before is not the best use of your time. So don't do any studying! This may be the only time you ever hear this again! Instead, we suggest you prepare in other ways, like:

- *Getting together a "Test Day Kit" containing the following items:*
  - *A calculator with fresh batteries*
  - *A watch*
  - *Five or more No. 2 pencils (pencils with slightly dull points fill the ovals better)*
  - *Erasers*
  - *Photo ID card (e.g., passport, driver's license, or student ID)*
  - *Your admission ticket*
  - *A snack—there are breaks, and you'll probably get hungry*
  - *A light coat*
- *Relax. Do some relaxation and visualization techniques.*
- *Read a magazine, take a long, hot shower, or watch something on TV.*
- *Get a good night's sleep.*

✓ The morning of the test:
First, wake up! After that:

- *Eat breakfast. Make it something substantial, but not anything too heavy or greasy.*

- *Don't drink a lot of coffee if you're not used to it. Bathroom breaks cut into your test time, and too much caffeine may make you jittery.*

- *Dress in layers so that you can adjust to the temperature of the testing room.*

- *Read something. Warm up your brain with a newspaper or a magazine. Don't let the test booklet be the first thing you read that day!*

- *Be sure to get there early. Allow yourself extra time for traffic, mass transit delays, or detours.*

Work Experience

A job in the real world can earn you some extra cash as well as show the college admissions folks that you can keep a commitment, manage time effectively, and determine priorities.

Who knows? You might also discover your future career or, at the very least, find out that you hate serving up lattes.

Getting a Job during School

Go to your local burger joint, mall, coffeehouse, etc., and ask if they need any help. If so, fill out an application. Consider applying for jobs that relate to your interests—maybe the physical therapy clinic needs a receptionist or the local newspaper is looking for an office assistant.

Just like with your extracurricular activities, it's a good idea to spend your time doing what you love. This table will give you an idea of how to link up your interests with a real-world job.

If you are interested in	Look for work at
Law	Legal firm, courthouse, law school legal clinics
Computers	Technology store, computer repair shop
Writing	Bookstore, library, newspaper, magazine
Education	Summer camp, your local community college
Fashion	Your favorite clothing store, fabric store
Science/Engineering	Pharmaceutical company, medical lab
Biology/Ecology	Zoo, aquarium, wildlife reserve, state park
Art	Museum, gallery
Medicine/Health Services	Hospital, doctor's office, public health outreach
Sports	Athletic office of a local college, recreation center
Music	Record store, recording studio, music magazine, band

One of the big perks of employment is the discounts—10 percent off CDs or books could really help your budget (and help you decide what to get people for their birthdays!). Plus, working gives you the opportunity to meet new people that you may not otherwise have a chance to encounter. And who knows, you could bump into your future prom date at work! If you perform well at work, you may be eligible for a raise!

Building Your Résumé

A high school résumé, activity résumé, or brag sheet is a document that describes your accomplishments: your school activities, your work and volunteer experience, and honors. It's an organized summary of your time spent outside of the classroom. It should communicate to a college what you have to offer them!

Not only should it list your activities, but it should also include your position (e.g., captain, president, etc.), the time you spent doing the activity (e.g., two hours a week/40 weeks a year), and a brief description of the activity. It's a great idea to give a copy of your résumé to each of your college recommenders when you ask him or her to write a letter of recommendation for you. The following are useful websites for building your college résumé:

- *www.collegeboard.com*
- *www.collegeconfidential.com*
- *www.petersons.com*

Résumé To-Dos

✓ List your most impressive and important activities first.

✓ Highlight specific details about your activities.

✓ Use active verbs to describe your roles, i.e., assisted, starred, led, participated, completed, performed, etc.

✓ Keep the page neat, organized, and easy to read. Ask for help with formatting if you need it.

✓ Spell out acronyms. Admissions officers don't know that WHSSC stands for Westborough High School Science Club.

✓ Give your résumé to teachers/counselors who are writing recommendation letters for you. It'll help them get a full handle on your accomplishments.

✓ Hand it to admissions counselors at the start of your interviews so they can ask you questions about your achievements.

✓ Send it along with every application.

College Is Close!

Questions to Ask Your Guidance Counselor

You're going to be seeing a lot of your guidance counselor this year! Here are some very important questions you should make sure to ask:

- "Can we go over my transcript and talk about my options?"
- "Do you have college catalogs and other resource books for me to use?"
- "What is my class rank?"
- "Am I eligible for fee waivers for standardized tests and college applications?"
- "What can you tell me about scholarships and financial aid?"
- "Can you help me fill out the FAFSA?"
- "What information do you need from me to write my recommendation when I apply to college?"
- "If I have a list of colleges that I want to apply to, do you have any other suggestions for other institutions that I should consider?"
- "Am I a good fit for the colleges on my list?"
- "What colleges are past students from this school attending? Do you know any students who are attending colleges on my list?"

Hey Athletes! Register with the NCAA

According to the National College Athletic Association (NCAA), only about 2 percent of students compete in Division I or Division II college sports. If you are in that small minority and are working toward being recruited by colleges, you will have to register with the NCAA Eligibility Clearinghouse (*www.ncaaclearinghouse.net*) and be certified as an amateur. The NCAA recommends that you register in your junior year.

You must also meet the academic requirements to qualify, which includes a minimum grade point average and required minimum score on the ACT or SAT. Division I schools are the most competitive and offer the largest scholarships. However, keep in mind that smaller schools may present more opportunities to play sports. Being recruited for the best football team in the country may mean little or no playing time.

If you love sports but are not a star athlete, there are plenty of other options to pursue your interests. The least competitive level of intercollegiate sports is at Division III schools, which offer no scholarships and focus on players instead of prestige. If you see sports purely as recreational, you can join an intramural team at your college. Intramural sports give students a chance to play their favorite sports on campus, without any pressure.

College Fair

Go where the admissions reps are—go to a college fair! Ask your guidance counselor when the next local fair is coming up. You can also go to the National Association for College Admission Counseling (NACAC) website (*www.nacacnet.org*) to find out when the next national fair in your area will be held.

These events can be a bit overwhelming—especially the biggies run by the NACAC—but with a little planning, you'll get all the info you need.

Before You Get There
- ✓ Look over the list of participants.
- ✓ Mark the colleges that you'd like to learn about.
- ✓ Write down a few questions for the college representatives.
- ✓ Print up some self-adhesive labels with your name, address, phone number, email

address, high school, graduation year, intended major (it's OK to put undecided), and any extracurricular activities you're interested in pursuing. These labels are particularly handy because, instead of filling out a ton of college information cards by hand, you can just stick your labels on the cards and spend more time learning about colleges.

✓ Stick your lists, labels, a pen, and a pad into a bag (a large one for all of the info you'll be bringing home) to take to the fair.

While You Are There

✓ Look for a map of where each college is located, and plan out a direct route so you'll have time to visit all the colleges on your list—grab all the brochures and catalogs you can carry.

✓ Write down a few thoughts about each college and the answers to your questions as soon as you leave a booth. Then move on to the next table on your route.

✓ Browse the colleges that didn't make it onto your list. Don't just stick to the booths that seem popular. You never know—a college you've never heard of might just be everything you're looking for.

✓ Start at the far end of the room; everyone begins talking to colleges near the entrance of the fair, so beat the crowds by working the room in reverse!

✓ Talk to admissions representatives. Indicate your interest in the college, and ask intelligent questions. When you are finished, ask the rep for a business card—he or she could be a valuable contact in the future.

✓ If available, check out an info session on financial aid or applying to colleges.

After It's Over

✓ Reread your notes and start plowing through all those brochures you collected.

✓ Make a list of the colleges that you're STILL interested in.

✓ Start scheduling some visits. (If you or your parents are members of AAA, they can help you design your college tours.)

✓ Email or write admissions officers that you met at the fair to thank them for sharing information with you and express your continued interest in their college.

Campus Visits

Most people go on campus visits between the end of junior year and the beginning of senior year (from May to late August/early September).

Avoid visiting a college during exam weeks or on weekends. Otherwise, you won't get an accurate picture of the place. If this is not possible, try to schedule a second visit when classes are in session. This way, you get to see the good, the bad, and the ugly while the place is in full swing.

See if you can schedule an informational interview with an admissions officer the same day you're touring the campus. And if they offer appointments, visit the financial aid office, too.

Dress in "business casual" clothing on your college visits. That means no jeans, no dirty old sneakers, no T-shirts—no exceptions! Even if you decide to wear a $150 T-shirt, are you going to say to the admissions officer you're meeting with for an interview, "Oh, by the way, this is an expensive T-shirt"? Not likely. First impressions are important.

First Visit Checklist

Stuff these things into your backpack the day of the tour—you just might need them!

- ✓ Notebook and pen
- ✓ Digital camera
- ✓ Campus map and catalog
- ✓ Bottle of water and a snack
- ✓ A list of places you don't want to miss
- ✓ Umbrella (if it's overcast)
- ✓ A bunch of questions

And if you like a college, visit the campus a second time . . . or as many times as you like!

Second Visit Checklist

- ✓ Don't walk around campus aimlessly. Use this checklist as a guide to get you in gear.
- ✓ Sit in on a class of a subject that interests you.
- ✓ Talk to a professor after class.
- ✓ Grab a coffee at the student union, and check out the college newspaper.
- ✓ Talk to some students. Ask them what they like and don't like about the college. Ask them what they do for fun on the weekends.
- ✓ Sit in an outdoor quad and people watch.
- ✓ Browse in the college bookstore.
- ✓ Walk or drive around the community surrounding the campus.
- ✓ Check out a dorm you didn't get to see your first time around.
- ✓ Spend the night in a dorm if the college allows.
- ✓ Imagine yourself as a student.
- ✓ Talk to people who are involved with your extracurricular activities—coaches, club advisors, theater directors, and orchestra/band leaders are great contacts!

This time, skip the guided tour and get down with the students! A second visit is also a great time to schedule that interview if you couldn't do it on the first trip: Smaller colleges often offer students the opportunity to sit down face-to-face with an admissions officer—in other words, they offer a college interview. Although a successful interview will not guarantee admission, it will put a face with your name, which will help you as admissions officers discuss your application. To schedule an appointment, call the admissions office AT LEAST three weeks in advance (make sure to get directions to the office!).

Attention Mom and Dad!

The campus visit is a highly personal experience. Let your child take the lead and ask the majority of questions. Limit yourself to no more than three questions; for example, it is perfectly appropriate to ask about financial aid, campus safety, and academic opportunities. Try to walk at least six steps behind the groups of students on the tour—let your child have the front seat!

Questions to Ask at Visits

Don't be shy! Ask your guide the scoop on:

- The best place to study (it might not be the library)
- The nicest dorms
- The coolest on-campus jobs
- The tastiest cafeteria food
- Where students hang out on campus
- Athletic games and events
- Upcoming concerts
- Celebrity speakers
- Whatever!

Stick around for a few minutes after the tour to talk to the tour guide. If you're lucky, you might get some insight on more personal things, such as:

- Making new friends
- Transitioning from high school classes to college course work
- How to learn in a not-so-intimate lecture hall
- Awesome and not-so-awesome professors
- Joining a fraternity or sorority

Campus Visit To-Dos

✓ Make sure to schedule a college visit when classes are in session.
This way, you get to see the good, the bad, and the ugly while the place is in full swing.

✓ Take a campus tour.
A student guide will not only show you around, he or she will also show you the personality of the campus so you can picture yourself living and learning there.

✓ Use your time wisely.
You can turn an average tour into an amazing one just by asking a few questions. Hey, you might even inspire other prospective students to inquire about things they never thought to ask.

✓ Dress code is business casual!
Do wear comfortable shoes, though, since you will be walking most of the day.

✓ Plan a three-in-one.
See if you can schedule an informational interview with an admissions officer the same day you're touring the campus. And if they offer appointments, visit the financial aid office, too.

Financial Aid in Grade 11

Financial Aid 101

Why bother doing the research if you KNOW you can't pay for it? Well, for one thing, who says YOU'RE going to pay for it all?

When it comes to financial aid, guidance counselors say that the biggest mistakes families make are applying too late or not applying at all. You can get money from various sources, including:

- College scholarships: The ones that want you to attend will most likely offer you some sort of financial aid package if you need it.

- Individual scholarships: Scholarship programs that donate funds based on criteria ranging from heritage to employment to what kind of toppings you like on your pizza.

- Federal and state grants: Uncle Sam wants you to go to college, too! Federal and state grants are there for the taking.

- Student loans: These can really help you in a bind. You do have to pay them back, though.

- Work-study programs: Many colleges offer these programs. You receive minimum wage in exchange for doing useful work on campus, like accepting packages of cheetah blood in the Anthropology department (not kidding!).

Apply for financial aid even if you think you won't get any. You've got to be in it to win it!

Financial Aid Terms You Should Know

Before we dive headfirst into the nitty-gritty, here are some financial aid terms you should come to know and love:

★ Balloon Payment: Paying off the outstanding balance of your loan without penalty.

★ College Scholarship Service (CSS) Profile: A nongovernment aid application that some colleges require.

★ Eligible Noncitizen: Someone who is not a U.S. citizen but is eligible for federal student aid.

★ Expected Family Contribution (EFC): This is the amount your family is expected to contribute, based on the FAFSA (see below).

★ Federal Work-Study (FWS): Need-based, part-time employment in college, where the federal government pays part of the student's salary, making it cheaper for departments and businesses to hire the student.

★ Free Application for Federal Student Aid (FAFSA): Form used to apply for Pell Grants and all other need-based aid. You can't get federally backed college assistance without this form!

★ Gift Aid: Money, such as grants and scholarships, which does not have to be repaid.

★ Graduated Repayment: A schedule where your monthly payments are smaller at the start of the repayment period, gradually becoming larger.

★ Grant: Money based on financial need that you do not have to repay.

★ Loan: Money that must be repaid with interest. The federal student loan programs (FFELP and FDSLP) can finance the costs of your college education at a lower interest rate than most consumer loans, without a credit check or collateral. Government-backed Stafford and Perkins loans provide a variety of deferment and repayment options.

★ Merit-Based Aid: Depending on your academic, artistic, or athletic merit.

★ Need-Based Aid: Depending on your financial need.

★ Pell Grants: Federal money for low-income students that you do not have to repay.

★ PLUS Loans: Government-backed loans given to parents.

★ Scholarships: Money from a college or a private source that you do not have to repay.

★ Subsidized Loans: Any government-backed loans where all the government pays all your interest while at school.

★ State Grants: Money a state gives resident students attending in-state schools.

★ Student Aid Report (SAR): Report summarizing FAFSA information that colleges use to define your aid package. The SAR indicates the amount of Pell Grant eligibility and the EFC.

★ Unsubsidized Loan: Any government-backed loan where the government does not pay interest on the loan while you are in school.

Need-Based Aid

As the term suggests, need-based aid looks at a family's financial resources to determine how much money the student needs to attend college. Examples are government-supported student loans and grants offered to low-income families.

Financial aid offices at colleges and universities look at your parents' income and financial situation to determine how much they should be able to contribute to your education (your "expected family contribution" or EFC). This involves a mathematical calculation referred to as need analysis. This need analysis will be done both by the federal government and the financial aid offices at each school to which you are applying.

Usually, the government calculates its need analysis for you, and then informs each of your potential colleges of its decision. This, in turn, may influence the need analysis calculated by those schools.

Federal Pell Grant

When filing financial aid forms with the federal government, you will be considered for a Pell Grant. It's the largest grant program offered by the federal government.

The amount in aid a student receives is based upon his or her need analysis and whether the student will attend college full- or part-time. Millions of students from low-income families receive Pell Grants each year, but the vast majority of middle-income families do not qualify for this aid.

Academic Competitiveness Grant

This federal grant was first introduced for the 2006–2007 academic year, and it provides up to $750 for the first year of undergraduate study and up to $1,300 for the second year. Students must be U.S. citizens, enrolled in full-time undergraduate study, and eligible for a Federal Pell Grant. Most important, students must have completed a rigorous high school program. Details are available at *www.studentaid.ed.gov*.

National SMART Grant

The National SMART (Science and Mathematics Access to Retain Talent) Grant provides up to $4,000 for each of the third and fourth years of undergraduate study for students majoring in physical, life, or computer sciences; math; technology engineering; or a foreign language that is critical to national security. As with the Academic Competitiveness Grant, students must be enrolled in full-time undergraduate study, U.S. citizens, and eligible for the Federal Pell Grant. Students must also have a GPA of at least 3.0 in their major.

Merit-Based Aid

Merit-based financial aid is not based on financial need but upon a student's achievements, ability, contributions, or potential, and is awarded regardless of the recipient's financial status. For example, athletic scholarships are merit-based aid, as are grants awarded to top academic students for their grades. Merit-based aid is usually awarded by colleges, organizations, or businesses and corporations.

The factors involved in awarding merit-based aid depend upon the school itself, as well as the type of aid given. If an academic scholarship pays for the tuition of a student who majors in biology and is a minority, qualifying students must not only have good grades, but they must obviously major in biology and be a minority. Not all merit-based aid is so narrow in scope.

Corporations may offer scholarships to students based solely on GPA or PSAT score, or a local organization may provide a grant to an exceptional student in the area. Scholarships and grants are also available based upon artistic talents and other abilities beyond academics and athletics.

Because of the nature of merit-based aid, colleges use these types of assistance to remain competitive with other schools. For example, a well-known state school with a good academic reputation may try to compete with Ivy League schools for top students. In this situation, the public school may offer to give a top student a free education in hopes of luring the student away from an Ivy League school. Keep an eye out for Honors Programs which are small, elite 'colleges within colleges'. Schools often offer special grants to attract the best talent to these programs. Likewise, schools may award scholarships to minorities in hopes of creating a more diverse student body.

Non-Need-Based/Non-Merit-Based Aid: Student Loans

The good news is that non-need-based and non-merit-based aid exists. The bad news is that it is primarily granted in the form of loans.

This aid is offered without any special stipulation regarding achievement or potential, and is granted irrespective of the family's financial status. The U.S Department of Education administers the Federal Family Education

Loan (FFEL) Program and the William D. Ford Federal Direct Loan (Direct Loan) Program, both commonly known as Stafford loans. The FFEL Program is often referred to as the Federal Stafford loan and the Direct Loan Program is referred to as the Direct Stafford loan. Most colleges participate in one program or the other; some colleges participate in both. Each can be subsidized or unsubsidized.

Similarly, any parent is eligible to apply for Parental Loans for Undergraduate Students (PLUS loans). These are federal loans for the parents of undergraduate students only. These unsubsidized loans are not need-based, so any parent is eligible. Repayment begins 60 days after the money is loaned, and parents can borrow up to the cost of the college (minus any financial aid). Fees are charged, and because lenders check the parent's credit history, a cosigner may be required or the loan may be denied if there are credit problems.

Perkins loans are need-based loans offered to students at 5 percent interest. Colleges have set funds designated for Perkins loans and select recipients to receive them. Interest on a Perkins loan does not accrue while the student is in college, and repayment doesn't begin until nine months after the student graduates. Undergraduate students can borrow up to $5,500 a year, depending on eligibility.

Work-Study Programs

Often called work-study programs, work aid is money earned by the student to help afford college.

Most colleges offer work-study programs, where you work on campus part-time. Depending upon the school or program, you may receive paychecks, or the money may be subtracted from your tuition and fees. The money will only be subtracted from tuition and fees if you opt to sign your paychecks over to the college.

The exact process for this option varies from school to school, so be sure to find out the details from the financial aid office if you plan to use a work-study program to cover a portion of your tuition.

Most work-study programs require students to work 10 to 15 hours a week during the semester. This is certainly a reasonable amount of time for you to work. However, in order to receive the full benefit of this program, you must be responsible and actually perform the work! Consider this option very carefully.

State Aid

Students with financial need should apply for both federal and state aid. Because each type of aid uses different formulas to determine eligibility, those who don't qualify for federal aid may still be eligible for state aid. According to the National Center for Public Policy and Higher Education, state and local governments currently provide $72 billion for college aid!

- If you hope to go to an in-state school, check out the school's website or financial aid office for their advice on what your state and local governments can offer.

- Apply early. Colleges tend to be more generous with the first few aid packages.

- All 50 states give merit- and need-based aid, and they can be more generous than the feds For links to your state's aid office, go to *www.studentaid.ed.gov.*

- State aid is usually offered to in-state school students. If you're going to another state's public university, research whether your state has a reciprocal or reduced out-of-state tuition rate. Such diverse states as Hawaii and Colorado have reciprocal reduced tuition agreements, so you might be pleasantly surprised! Aloha!

Different states have different application procedures. If you decide to apply for state aid, speak with your guidance counselor or contact your state's agency to learn more about the forms that need to be filled out. Go for it!

Army ROTC

Army ROTC (or the Army Reserve Officers' Training Corps) is a program you take along with your required college classes and is basically a fast track to becoming an officer in the United States Army. During school, you will take training and leadership courses as a cadet, and upon graduation, you will be a second lieutenant. There are many extraordinary opportunities afforded to you by participating in the ROTC program, including exceptional career development assistance.

Army ROTC offers merit-based scholarships to high school students. The Four-Year Scholarship for high school students is for those people planning on attending and completing a four-year college program. In order to qualify for the ROTC program and the scholarship, you must meet certain requirements. These requirements stipulate that you:

- Be a U.S. citizen
- Be between the ages of 17 and 26
- Have a high school cumulative GPA of at least 2.50
- Score minimum of 920 on the SAT (math/verbal) or 19 on the ACT (excluding the required Writing Test scores)
- Meet physical standards
- Agree to accept a commission and serve in the Army on Active Duty or in a Reserve Component (U.S. Army Reserve or Army National Guard)

Some schools may have ROTC for other branches of the military as well such as the Navy. Talk to your guidance counselor if you'd like to find out more, or visit *www. goarmy.com*.

Books on Aid

Check out these books with financial aid tips at your library or bookstore:

- *Kaplan Scholarships: Billions of Dollars in Free Money for College*, by Gail Schlachter and R. David Weber, Kaplan
- *Free $ for College for Dummies*, by David Rosen and Caryn Mladen, For Dummies
- *How to Go to College Almost for Free*, by Ben Kaplan, Collins

Handbooks and Magazines on Aid

Your neighborhood reference librarian or bookseller can lead you to these handbooks and magazines:

Handbooks

- *U.S. News & World Report. America's Best Colleges*
- *College Money Handbook*, Peterson's

Magazines

- *Key*
- *Kiplinger's Personal Finance*
- *Money*
- *Reason*
- *SmartMoney*
- *USA Today Financial Aid*

Download U.S. government publications "Student Guide, Funding Your Education," at http://studentaid. ed.gov/sites/default/files/2012-13-funding-your-education.pdf.

Websites on Aid

Do some more financial aid research online!

- *www.ed.gov*
- *www.fafsa.ed.gov*
- *www.finaid.org*
- *www.fastweb.com*

Social Networking in Grade 11

Network, Network, Network

It's never too early to network for internships, future jobs, and colleges. Social networking sites can be used to form connections and get information, whether it's study tips, college application to-dos, or career advice.

Use Facebook to Find Colleges

Even Facebook can help you manage the college admissions process. Many college admissions offices have their own Facebook page. You can find out more about your top choice schools—what they have to offer and what they're looking for. You can get information about requirements, open houses, campus tours, application deadlines, and contact information, all in one place.

It gives you instant access to the admissions office in the event that you have a question. For example, you may want to ask if tickets to a campus event are available. This shows that you're interested in the school and will likely be active in campus life. It shows you took the time to learn what that school has to offer and that you're serious about attending.

But use that Facebook account wisely. Don't harass them!

Facebook To-Dos

- Form study groups with peers, to help tackle that dreaded SAT or AP exam.

- Get advice from students who have taken the same classes or have gone through the same programs.

- Join groups at your school, such as a club or the honor society.

- Research scholarship, internship, or college programs.

- Join college admissions pages to get contact information, learn about requirements and dead-lines, or schedule campus visits and tours.

- Network! Your Facebook friends can be a great resource to connect you to jobs and colleges.

Summer, Summer, Summertime

The Summer before Grade 12

✓ Start preparing for the SAT an/or ACT.
Take a practice exam to identify your strengths and weaknesses. If you have trouble taking tests or want to improve your chances of getting a high score, sign up for a test prep course. Almost every student who purchased a test prep guide will tell you that they wish they had started studying earlier. If you start early, you may only need to devote 15–20 minutes a day to studying.

✓ Visit colleges.
If you're going on a trip with your family, find out what colleges are in the area and arrange to take a campus tour. Or you can make special trips just to visit colleges. Don't forget to pick up applications and other information wherever you go.

✓ Consider a summer residential program at a college.
  These programs can be really intense experiences, with a variety of classes, sports, trips, and social activities. For students who want to spend the summer away from home and get a taste of life on a college campus, residential programs may be just the thing.

✓ Look for free options for cultural enrichment.
  Summer is the time for all kinds of cultural festivals, including outdoor concerts, dance performances, and fairs, which are almost always free. Also, make sure to check with your local city parks department for similar kinds of activities.

✓ If you are artistically inclined, look for a summer arts program.
  You may be able to find one at your local YMCA, community center, or college.

✓ Learn a foreign language or improve on what you already know.
  A number of colleges offer foreign language immersion programs during the summer.

✓ Keep reading, writing, and traveling!

Chapter 5:
Grade 12

You're almost there! You've researched schools, narrowed down your list, and taken all of those big tests. All that's left is to put together your application materials, send them in, and wait for the good news.

This year is a great time to look back and celebrate everything you've achieved, but you also need to stay on top of both college admissions and your schoolwork. Applying to college can be a messy process, with lots of little odds and ends, so pay attention to the tips in this chapter to help you stay organized.

Once you've selected a school, it's time to start thinking about the logistics of setting up your life on a college campus. Read on for advice and resources on banking, insurance, finding a doctor, shopping for college, and all the other bases you'll need to cover in order to feel at home when you settle in next fall. And if you don't initially get the news you were hoping for, learn how you can best deal with being wait listed by your top choice.

Finally, it's important to keep up your momentum—and your academic performance—even after you've been accepted. This chapter will also give you some helpful hints for avoiding "senioritis."

Grade 12 To-Dos

Senior year has arrived and you're finally in the home stretch! College is not that far off, yet there's still a ton for you to do. Most important, you need to apply to college! Most guidance counselors want to help you, but they can't help if you don't fill them in on your plans.

Plan, Plan, Plan

✓ Check in with your guidance counselor early on.

✓ If applicable, take or retake the SAT and/or ACT, as well as any Subject Tests.

✓ Finalize your college list. Be sure to include some reach and some safety schools. Remember, your goal is to get into the best schools for you!

✓ Filling out college applications might seem like a full-time job, so stay organized and keep track of deadlines, especially if you plan to apply early action or early decision.

✓ Check in with your recommenders. Be sure they have all the information on you that they need.

Academics

✓ You may have heard this a million times, but now is not the time to slack off!
Keep up with your schoolwork. Senior grades do count! In fact, some colleges wait to see either first quarter or first semester grades before making their admission decision.

Extracurricular

✓ Keep on doing what you love!

Other Tips

✓ Keep on top of financial aid. Some schools require a CSS Profile (in addition to the FAFSA, which you will submit in January). Check with the schools to which you're applying.

✓ If you got in early decision—congrats! Remember to withdraw your other applications.

✓ If you didn't get in early decision or early action, be sure to keep track of your regular-decision deadlines.

✓ Submit the FAFSA.

✓ Ask your counselor to send your midyear grades to the schools to which you're applying.

✓ Prepare for any AP tests that you plan on taking in May.

✓ If you applied under regular decision, hang in there—you should receive a decision by April.

✓ Finally, it's time to make your decision. Most colleges have a May 1 commitment deadline. Too many offers? Make another campus visit.

The Last Leg of the Race!

Avoid Senioritis

What exactly IS senioritis? Senioritis (seen-yoor-i-tiss) is the quality or state of being totally uninterested in the academic portion of high school, usually suffered by graduating seniors. It's the desire to goof off in class, spend hours on Facebook, and/or create a masterful plot to kidnap the opposing football team's mascot at the expense of studying for finals.

It is VERY important that you avoid senioritis at all costs, even if you've already received an acceptance letter from your top college choice. Many colleges make your admission offer conditional on maintaining your GPA. If it drops significantly, you might just get another letter telling you to stop packing.

Don't worry, though. It's easy to avoid the 'itis. Here's a checklist to keep you on track:

✓ Take challenging classes that will prepare you for college course work.

✓ Stay involved in your school and community service activities.

✓ Consider an internship to start you on a possible career track.

✓ Start planning and packing for college.

✓ Read. You will most likely be required to read some classic literature your freshman year of college—why not get a jump on it? For starters, you can try:

- *Crime and Punishment,*
  Fyodor Dostoevsky, 1866

- *One Hundred Years of Solitude,*
  Gabriel García Márquez, 1967

- *The Catcher in the Rye,*
  J. D. Salinger, 1951

- *Maus: A Survivor's Tale,*
  Art Spiegelman, 1992

- *1984,*
  George Orwell, 1949

- *Their Eyes Were Watching God,*
  Zora Neale Hurston, 1937

- *Dubliners,*
  James Joyce, 1914

- *Hiroshima,*
  John Hersey, 1946

- *Pride and Prejudice,*
  Jane Austen, 1813

- *Hamlet,*
  William Shakespeare, ca. 1601

- *A Doll's House,*
  Henrik Ibsen, 1879

Some of these books your professors will expect you to have covered in high school, some are guaranteed to be on the syllabi of introductory courses in your major, and some are simply stimulating reads that will help you to develop a more well-rounded knowledge of classic literature (and that won't hurt, no matter what your major).

✓ Don't designate every Friday as senior cut day.

✓ Don't slack off on homework and studying.

✓ Don't forget to enjoy the time you have left with your friends and teachers. You won't be a high school student much longer!

College Classes Now

Admissions counselors look for rigorous, demanding courses. Taking college-level courses is one of the best ways to give you an edge on the competition. However, be aware that every college and every department has a different policy when it comes to accepting transfer credits.

Most colleges offer courses that are open to high school students as long as you pay tuition. An increasing number of institutions have online courses as well. Such classes are generally open to juniors and seniors. You can also look into options for the summer, when many colleges host residential programs for high school students. Depending on which college you choose, these programs can be very expensive.

Dual enrollment initiatives allow students the opportunity to earn college credits while still in high school. When looking for information on the Web, run "dual enrollment" and your state name through a search engine to find out what colleges offer these programs near you. Many of these programs offer college classes for free; however, tuition policies vary from state to state. Dual enrollment programs often require a certain minimum GPA to participate.

Financial Aid in Grade 12

Luckily for you, you've done a lot of background research on financial aid already. Now, here are some tips on filing for aid and evaluating the packages you get!

Free Application for Federal Student Aid (FAFSA)

The Free Application for Federal Student Aid (FAFSA) is the basic form required to apply for any federal financial aid. The FAFSA form is what you use to provide income tax information to the government. In turn, those numbers are used in the government's need-analysis process to decide how much your expected family contribution (EFC) will be, as well as how much aid you can receive. When filing the FAFSA, your information can be forwarded to potential colleges, which will help in their financial aid process. A new FAFSA must be completed every year and is required by all colleges.

Thanks to the Internet, you have a few options as to how you fill out this VERY important form. Most high school guidance offices offer the paper form, or you can request one by calling the Federal Student Aid Information Center at 800-4-FED-AID.

The easiest and fastest way to complete the FAFSA is online at *www.fafsa.ed.gov*. An added benefit to completing the form online is that if you need to make a correction after the FAFSA has been processed, you can do so online. You will also be able to complete the renewal FAFSA online each year, instead of starting the process from scratch!

After your FAFSA is processed, you will receive a Student Aid Report (SAR) in the mail. This tells you the results of your need analysis and lets you know how much your EFC is. This same information will be reported to your prospective colleges. Your EFC is not negotiable, so even if the amount is more than you can afford, there is no way to change this number (unless some of your information is incorrect and you correct those amounts on your FAFSA).

CSS PROFILE

In addition to the FAFSA, some schools will ask you to submit a second application, the CSS/Financial Aid PROFILE®, for nonfederal (private) aid. These schools will use your PROFILE application to help them award scholarships and grants that are given out by the school. (Be sure to complete a FAFSA, too, since it's the only way you will be considered for federal aid.)

The PROFILE requires most of the same information you will submit for a FAFSA but also asks about additional factors like trust funds and high school tuition expenses. This gives colleges a more complete picture of your family's financial situation.

To learn more about the application, see a list of participating schools, or submit an application, visit the official CSS/Financial Aid PROFILE site at *http://profileonline.collegeboard.com.*

Comparing Financial Aid Packages

The amount offered to students is often called a financial aid package. This package is the amount of financial aid you will receive, minus grants and scholarships. Ideally, your financial aid package will cover the complete amount of money you'll need to afford college (in other words, whatever the difference is between the cost of this college and what you can afford to pay). Unfortunately, this is seldom the case.

When the combination of your financial aid package and the amount you can pay falls short of the cost of that college, you're faced with a few choices. When this happens, you and your parents may decide to take out loans to cover this difference. Other options are that you try to reduce the cost of this college further or decide not to attend this particular college.

But remember! An informed decisions on how to proceed will be based on ALL your prospective colleges, not just one award letter! Because your prospective colleges cost different amounts, these schools are going to have calculated different amounts of need in order for you to attend. Because of this, you might assume that private and out-of-state colleges are going to provide you with more financial aid than a local public school. Yet you may be surprised by the award letters you receive.

The first thing you'll probably do when you receive each financial aid package is review the big picture—in other words, you'll immediately look to see if the amount of financial aid being offered is going to be enough. If it's not, then this is what colleges call your "unmet need."

"Gapping" is another term for this difference, and it's the difference between your need (as calculated by the college) and the amount of financial aid they offer you. If a college determines your need to be $8,000 a year, but your aid package only offers $5,000 in financial aid, then your unmet need is $3,000.

Remember that colleges determine your need by subtracting your EFC from the cost of attending that college, so different amounts of unmet need are not going to necessarily reflect the dollar amount of your aid package. For example, let's say you apply to your dream school and a safety school. The dream school may offer a $12,000 aid package, while the safety school offers a $4,000 aid package. At first, the dream school may look like the better choice, but what if that dream school is going to cost $20,000 a year, while you could attend the safety school for only $6,000 a year?

Even with this significant difference in financial aid offers, the unmet need for your dream school would be $8,000 a year, while the unmet need for the safety school would be only $2,000 a year. This difference alone shouldn't be the deciding factor in which college you will attend, but it will tell you how much you'd actually pay to attend various colleges. Deciding the impact of those differences will be up to you.

Appealing Aid Packages

As you compare your financial aid packages, you may notice a significant difference between colleges. Let's say that one school offers you a need-based grant for low-income families, and that this grant will pay for most of the cost of that college, but the college you really want to attend didn't offer any kind of grant at all. Not too long ago, families were stuck with what they were offered.

Today, it's becoming more and more common for families to negotiate their financial aid. Many parents argue that if schools want to compete for students, they should be willing to reconsider a financial aid package if another college has made a significantly better offer. This attitude is slowly changing the financial aid process, and you'll find that colleges react to this differently. Some actually encourage parents to provide them with offers from competing colleges so they can attempt to improve a student's aid. Other schools refuse to reconsider their package, insisting the quality of the education and the reputation of the college make up for the difference in financial aid. Most, however, fall somewhere in the middle and are willing to listen, assuming the college overlooked something or that your financial situation has changed.

If you decide to negotiate your financial aid package, you or your parents will need to be prepared before contacting the school. First of all, make sure you have a legitimate reason for asking a college to reconsider their financial aid package. Treat the process as if you're making a request because really that's what you're doing. Having a negative, angry attitude and insisting that a college increase their aid will destroy any chance of being successful. You may choose to call the financial aid office or write a letter making your request. Whichever method you chose, be sure to do the following:

- Remind the school that you are interested in attending (if you weren't interested, you wouldn't be asking them to do this). If the school is your first choice, state this!

- Ask if there is a possibility that you can receive more help with expenses (preferably a grant).

- Give a specific reason for your request (maybe another college offered a low-income grant, or one of your parents was recently forced to take a pay cut at his or her job). If you mention another school's offer, be up front and honest. Explain how you qualified for that particular aid and ask if this college had considered you for something similar.

- Acknowledge that you appreciate the person's time and consideration and that they are welcome to contact you if they have questions.

Financial Aid To-Dos

✓ Request the CSS PROFILE and FAFSA forms either on paper or get them online.
If you want to file your FAFSA online, request a pin number from www.pin.ed.gov.

✓ Don't wait until summer to file your FAFSA.
File it as soon as possible after January 1. You can always make changes to it later, but schools need your FAFSA as soon as possible if you don't want to miss the deadlines for certain aid opportunities.

✓ Ask your parents to file their taxes in January instead of April.

This way you can send in the FAFSA way earlier than the rest of the financial aid seekers, and you'll have a good shot at a better package.

✓ Complete and submit the CSS PROFILE form (if necessary).

✓ Complete any state, institutional, and other financial aid forms necessary.

Find out the filing deadlines for the FAFSA and CSS PROFILE with your prospective schools.

✓ Review your acknowledgment letters from various programs, and submit additional information for verification (if necessary).

✓ Review your financial aid packages with your parents, compare them, and determine the best course of action.

Applying to Colleges

Applications

Once you've got your final, definitive list of schools you'd like to go to, it's time to apply. Contact the admissions offices for those schools, or go to the schools' website to find out their application policies and procedures.

These days, you should be able to apply to most schools online instead of with the old-school paper application through the mail. If you do end up submitting a paper application, remember to type everything! Handwritten applications are often tossed to the side because they are too difficult to read.

There will be a list of required documentation to go along with your application, such as transcripts, recommendation letters, test score results, and the like. Be sure to read the applications thoroughly, and get all the supplemental materials they ask for as early as possible!

The Common Application

Filling out applications for the countless colleges that you're aiming for can be a mind-numbingly painful and repetitive process. It often seems like you're just repeating the same information over and over again. If you're lucky, most schools you are applying to accept the Common Application. It's a single application for undergraduate college admission used by a consortium of colleges and universities. There are currently 488 member colleges and universities, both public and private, that agree to give full consideration to applications submitted on this one common form.

Because so many schools participate, the Common Application can simplify the admissions process. Several colleges even use the Common Application as their own form! Not sure if your target school is one of them? You can find the member list on the Common Application website, *www.commonapp.org.*

There are two different ways of using the form: on paper or online. Using the paper form (available in your guidance office or by downloading from *www.commonapp.org*), you complete one Common Application, photocopy it, and send it to any of the member colleges to which you want to apply. Using the electronic version, you may either submit your application via the Internet or print it and mail a hard copy.

Do keep in mind, though, that some colleges require a supplemental form of their own. At *www.commonapp.org*, you can access supplemental forms to complete online and links to downloadable forms on individual college websites.

Forgetting $omething?

Did you pay your application fee online? No? Well, remember to SEND YOUR CHECK to the college! Yes? Print out the confirmation for proof of payment!

Transcripts

Colleges you want to apply to must receive your transcript—in other words, hard, cold proof, in writing, of your sparkling 4.0 GPA. But you can't just give them a photocopy of your report card. You must request that your high school send them an official transcript directly.

But don't expect your high school to forward your transcript overnight—especially if you go to a large school. Request it early! Keep forgetting to ask the office to send out your transcript? Try these little reminders:

- Scatter reminder stickies on your bedroom mirror, your backpack, the fridge, the windshield of your car, etc.
- Tie ribbons to your pinkie in your favorite college colors to jog your memory.
- LAST RESORT! Ask your mom to send you a text message during your lunch period to remind you to do it then.

If you are delivering your applications online, remember to ask your guidance counselor to forward your transcript and letters of recommendation, too! Forgetting to do so is a common mistake among students. Don't let it happen to you!

Deadlines

Some colleges have rolling admissions, which means that they accept applications on a continuous basis up to a certain deadline. One major advantage of rolling admissions is that you are notified of the college's decision soon after you apply, rather than waiting until March or April, when other colleges send out notifications.

Even though the application deadline is more relaxed, don't wait until the last minute. Generally, financial aid and housing are still given out on a first-come, first-served basis. While federal aid (including loans) will be available (if you file the FAFSA), scholarships are limited. In addition, some colleges (especially large universities) have a limited amount of on-campus housing, so you may find yourself scrambling for a place to live.

Early Decision

You know that rumor about students gaining an edge by applying to a college early decision? It's true! Early decision means you apply in the fall and hear the good news by winter break. Colleges tend to accept more early decision applicants because the students who apply under early decision programs are usually of exceptionally high quality and are certain to attend. That's because they have to . . . or ELSE! Consider the following questions before you send in an early decision application:

- "Do I REALLY want to go to this college?"
  If accepted, you are bound to attend and cannot change your mind.

- "Do I want to apply to other colleges, too?"
  You're not allowed to if you're applying early decision.

- "Do I fit the academic profile of the college?"
  If not, then early decision probably won't help your chances of getting in.

- "Am I ready to apply to OTHER colleges if I'm

NOT accepted under early decision?" If you are not accepted under early decision, you will automatically be considered as a regular-decision applicant. That you selected to apply to a college under early decision shows a sincere interest in the college, so you may get brownie points during the regular application review; but remember, you are NOT guaranteed a spot, so you should apply to other colleges just in case.

What to Do If You Miss the Application Deadline

If you maintain organized files and schedule your application process carefully, you won't be late! There are a few options out there if you are:

- Try contacting the colleges. If they haven't already received tons of applications, you might be able to convince them to take yours late. If so, you'd better be ready to hand in your stuff ASAP.

- Check out colleges that have rolling admission. They may be all booked, but it can't hurt to look. You can find out which colleges offer rolling admission by visiting a college search engine such as *www.collegeboard.com* or *www.fastweb.com*.

- Go to the NACAC website. The National Association for College Admission Counseling publishes a *Space Availability Survey* in late May. Visit *www.nacac.com* often for updates.

- Think about community college. Depending on how much room is available, you may be able to enroll as late as the first week of classes. Almost all schools accept transfer students.

- Research colleges that offer January admissions. And make sure you don't miss THIS deadline!

Application Tips and Tricks

Knowing "the tricks" can only get you so far. You're always better off being yourself than trying to beat the system. For instance, applying to a program that's considered "easier to get into," rather than the one that you're truly interested in, can backfire. So think of the following as insider tips rather than tricks:

- Keep your mouth shut about where you're applying. Too many applicants from your high school cuts down your chances of being accepted.

- Let the colleges know you're really interested. Make personal connections with the college representative for your school and keep in touch. Many colleges consider "demonstrated interest" when making decisions.

- Send a thank-you note after interviews, visits, or if an admissions officer has been extremely helpful. You'll get your name in front of them again. When they're reading your application they'll feel as if they know you.

- Go beyond the brochure, website, and info session when answering a "Why this college?" essay. Do research and find out things that relate specifically to your goals. Show the college that you're a great match!

- Market yourself! If you do something special (art, music, photography) send a sample of your work.

- Submit additional information if necessary. If you have a special circumstance (e.g., a disability, parent's divorce, death in the family, etc.) that has affected your high school record, let the college know.

- Proofread your application. Careless mistakes show a lack of attention to detail, which is the last impression you want to give an admissions committee.

- Practice for interviews. This will make you less nervous and better prepared.

- If you don't need financial aid—let the college know.

The Essay

The college essay, or personal statement, is part of every college application form. It offers you the opportunity to set yourself apart from the rest of the competition—to distinguish yourself from the thousands of other applicants who have similar grades and test scores. But how do you accomplish that? Show them what you've learned, what's important to you, and how you think. This is your chance to color the reader's interpretation of the objective data included elsewhere in the application. Most important, your essay must ring true; your goal is to write an essay that reflects your attitudes, your values, and your perceptions of yourself. Above all, write your essay in your own voice—to do otherwise can be spotted very easily and could disqualify you from being admitted.

Think your essay has to be the most polished and perfect piece of writing ever? Think again! The admissions folks aren't looking for Shakespeare, they want to hear from the REAL you. Show them your unique qualities and accomplishments.

Five Tips to an Excellent Essay

1) **Write it yourself:** It's OK to have someone make suggestions on how to improve your essay, but in the end, the writing has to be all you, baby.

2) **Use your own voice:** Grammar is important, but admissions officers don't expect your prose to be supersophisticated BEFORE you're admitted to their colleges—only after you graduate.

3) **Be an individual:** Don't write what you THINK they want to hear. What are you, psychic? Besides, admissions officers can get pretty bored reading the same tired essay topic over and over.

4) **Think small:** That's right. Narrow down your statement from, say, how we can achieve world peace to something like how you used diplomacy to stop your little brother from throwing water balloons at your dates.

5) **Make it personal:** Reveal some kind of personal growth, deeply held value, or unique interest by focusing on a particular event in your life. You can write about the moment you realized you wanted to be a doctor, the lessons you learned at a job or internship, a relationship that changed your life, or any topic that demonstrates insight and growth.

Avoid Essay Traps

There's no such thing as a perfect essay, but you can avoid some dangerous traps—if you know what they are.

- Don't write a boring first sentence. College admissions officers pore through thousands of essays, and they'll be more likely to read past the first sentence of yours if it's an attention grabber.
- Don't focus on others. Colleges want to learn about YOU. Unless you are specifically asked to write about someone else, don't.
- Don't use clichés. Nothing makes an essay reader more frustrated than having to read the same expression over and over.

- Don't get weird in order to seem creative. You do want to take a creative approach to an essay topic, but you don't want to cross the line into bizarre.

- Don't use flowery, artificial language. It just says, "Trying too hard."

- Don't procrastinate. Waiting until the last minute is a surefire way to sabotage a powerful essay.

- Don't whine. Nobody wants to hear someone complain.

- Don't restate your résumé. A laundry list of extracurricular activities does not offer interesting insights into your life and dreams.

- Don't be repetitive. Communicate your points once and well.

- Don't plagiarize. The admissions people know about all the college essay websites and books that have tons of essays. You will most likely get caught—as well as rejected.

Websites and Books on College Essays

For more essay advice, the following websites and books may be useful:

Websites

- *www.essayedge.com*
- *www.collegeboard.com*
- *www.myessay.com*
- *www.admissionsessays.com*

Books

- *Fiske Real College Essays That Work,* by Edward Fiske

- *On Writing the College Application Essay: The Key to Acceptance and the College of Your Choice,* by Harry Bauld

- *The College Application Essay*, by Sarah Myers McGinty
- *50 Successful Harvard Application Essays: What Worked for Them Can Help You Get into the College of Your Choice*, by *The Harvard Crimson*

How to Get Good Recommendations

There's a right way and a wrong way to acquire recommendations. Here are the dos and don'ts:

- Do get recommendations from teachers who KNOW you well and who can WRITE well. A glowing review from your favorite math guru doesn't pack a punch if he can't put a sentence together.
- Do make sure your references are relevant. If you want to major in marine biology, it might be best to ask a science or math teacher to write one.
- Do ask early—and give your recommender at least two weeks to write it. If you know for sure who you want to ask, start dropping hints at the end of junior year . . . they may want to write your letter during summer break!
- Do create a "cheat sheet" to help teachers write about you. List accomplishments, goals, and the colleges you'd like to attend. Give it (and your activity résumé) to your recommender before he or she writes your letter.
- Do send thank-you notes! The handwritten kind, not a mass email.
- Don't ask the popular teacher who doesn't know you very well.
- Don't wait until the last minute to ask and then expect it done ASAP.

- Don't pressure a teacher to write one when it's clear he or she doesn't want to do it.
- Don't forget to thank your recommenders.

Tips for Successful Interviews

The college interview offers you an opportunity to exchange or interact with an admissions officer. For the student, an interview provides a chance to highlight strengths and interests and to gather additional information about the college. For the admissions officer, it is a way to get to know the student and add to the personal and academic information that comprises an application file.

Here are some tips to help you do your best!

✓ Review the literature about the college before the interview.
At the very least, you want to appear knowledgeable about the school and keenly interested to learn more.

✓ Be prepared for common questions!
Admissions officers might throw you a curveball to see how you'll react in the interview. Be prepared! Here are ten tricky questions they sometimes ask. Prepare and rehearse your answers to these questions before your interview:

  ○ *What was the worst decision you've ever made?*

  ○ *How would your friends characterize you?*

  ○ *What is your biggest regret about high school, and if you could change it, what impact would it have on you and in your future as a college student?*

  ○ *If you were a world leader, what would you do to heal the violence and turbulence in the world?*

○ *How do you see yourself 20 years from now?*

○ *Who is the most influential person in your life and why?*

○ *What are you reading right now?*

○ *What makes you qualified to attend this college?*

○ *What will be your greatest challenge in college?*

○ *What separates this university from others?*

✓ Have your own questions ready!
Some students say that the hardest question you'll get from the interviewer is, in fact, "Do YOU have any questions?" Don't be caught off guard. You should definitely have some questions prepared. Questions about access to facilities, activities, off-campus programs, housing—or whatever is important to you!— are encouraged, and again, it shows your interest in the school. Write down your questions on a notepad that you will take with you to the interview.

✓ Bring along your notepad, a copy of your school transcript, and a brief résumé.
The notepad has your interview questions, but it's also there so you can take notes. You won't be able to remember everything, after all. The transcript and your résumé will come in handy if you are given an information sheet to fill out prior to your meeting. You won't have to scramble to remember things. It'll all be right there!

Pet Peeves of College Admissions Officers

You never know what could make an admissions officer banish your application to the reject pile. But these are some SUREFIRE ways to get rejected:

- Late applications!
- Sloppy/illegible handwriting—how can they evaluate something if they can't read it?
- Incomplete applications or forgetting to forward high school transcripts.
- Plagiarism
- Endless essays. Straying a bit from the word count is OK, but a ten-page essay is a definite no-no
- Typos and grammatical errors
- Fluorescent paper or other obvious attempts "to stand out"
- Using pencil or red or scented ink
- Too many recommendation letters—two or three are sufficient; 20 is going overboard
- Unsolicited videotapes and other media products when there's no time to view them

On the other hand, here are some things that make admissions officers smile:

- Students who follow directions—sending only requested materials and answering each essay question to the best of their ability
- An application with personality—they want to feel as though they know you after they've read it.
- Glowing and personalized letters of recommendation
- Essays that reflect a student's passions, interests, or personality

- Students who know why they want to attend a particular college—and it's not just because it has a "big name."

- Follow-up calls to ensure that all application materials have arrived

- Thank-you letters

Application To-Dos

✓ Make a checklist of the colleges that you plan to apply to.
Include columns to record the application deadline, financial aid deadline, and application fee. Check to see if any of your choices accept the Common Application (see www.commonapp.org). If they do, make sure to obtain the supplementary applications (if required) for each college as soon as possible. Some are available on the Common Application site, while others must be submitted through the college's own website.

✓ Get your recommendation letters out of the way as soon as you can.
Later in the process, teachers will be swamped with requests. Make sure that yours is one of the first. If applying electronically, print out copies of the recommendation forms and fill them out for your teacher (remember to type everything!) with all of the relevant information. Do the same with the paper application. Include an addressed, stamped envelope with each request.

✓ Fill out your transcript requests as soon as you decide where you're applying.
Don't be part of the rush later on!

✓ Keep copies of everything!
  If you apply electronically, make sure to print out every page of your application. If you must submit a paper application, make photocopies.

✓ If sending your applications through the mail, make sure that you purchase certified mail or delivery confirmation.
  Keep all postal receipts stapled to your application copies. You may need proof that you submitted your application by the deadline.

✓ Follow up if you need to!
  Wait a few days and then call the admissions office to confirm that they have all of your materials.

College Application Chart

Keep track of your college applications each step of the way. Use the following as a model for your chart of college applications—noting each college's admissions requirements and deadlines, as well as what you have already completed and sent out. Include dates, too!

College Name	_____	_____	_____
Website Address	_____	_____	_____
Application Deadline	_____	_____	_____
Financial Aid Deadline	_____	_____	_____
Accepts Common Application?	_____	_____	_____
Required Tests	_____	_____	_____
Academics?	_____	_____	_____
Essay Topic/ Length	_____	_____	_____
Recommendations	_____	_____	_____
Application Fee	_____	_____	_____
Date Sent	_____	_____	_____
Follow-Up Call	_____	_____	_____
Campus Tour	_____	_____	_____
Interview	_____	_____	_____
Thank-You Note	_____	_____	_____
Senior Year Grades/ Honors Sent	_____	_____	_____
Additional Test Scores Sent	_____	_____	_____

Social Networking in Grade 12

Many college staff members and professors have Facebook accounts that they use to network and connect with students. Also, more and more colleges are using Facebook to put accepted students in touch with each other before school starts. This is a great way to get in touch with current or former students to ask them questions about everything from academics to campus life. You can find out what it would take to join the college radio station or newspaper, for example.

As you apply to colleges, keep in mind that everyone from teachers who are writing your recommendations to college counselors and potential employers may be looking at your social networking sites.

Facebook To-Dos

- Find out more about school academic programs.
- Find out more about school admissions requirements.
- Find out more about school extracurricular offerings.
- Join groups at your top schools: the college basketball team, honor society, or student union, for example. Get key information about student life before getting there.
- Join your high school alumni association page. This can put you in touch with alumni who can guide you on the road to college and share their experiences and advice.
- Network with current and former students.
- Get course and professor recommendations.
- Meet new college friends!

Choosing Your College

I'm Wait-Listed!

If you were wait-listed, you met the basic requirements for the college, but you were not close enough to the top to guarantee your admission. Your first step is to contact the college to find out where you are on the list. You can also ask the admissions office if there is anything you can do to improve your chances. They may suggest that you submit further materials such as recommendations; they will certainly recommend that your final grades be as exceptional as possible.

If you are wait-listed for your first choice, take a second look at the colleges that already accepted you. You will not receive positive notification from the college where you were wait-listed until after deadlines for other colleges have passed.

I Want Deferred Admission

At some point in the college application process, you may decide that you're not ready to go to college yet. Maybe you want to work for a year to save up some money. Or you're thinking about traveling around the world by canoe. By selecting deferred admission, you can make that choice without giving up the chance to attend the college of your dreams.

Once you are accepted, you can approach the admissions office about deferring your enrollment until the next year. Make sure that you don't forget to submit any necessary paperwork or fail to send in your deposit! The success of your request may depend on how you present yourself and your reasons for taking time off.

Community Colleges Are Not Just for "Safety"!

The great thing about community college is that it's flexible. Whether you're still in high school or you're not so sure about your academic skills, you can find out if you're college material by taking just one class. If you need a little extra help, you'll be in the right place. Many community colleges offer small class sizes, where you'll find all the personal attention you need.

It's also a stepping-stone. You can attend a community college for a year or two, then transfer to a four-year university to gain a bachelor's degree. Some programs may even guarantee admission to a four-year school following your associates. Or maybe you want to go for a two-year associate's degree or graduate from a certificate program that will train you for the workforce. A community college just might be the ticket!

Plus, can you say "debtless education"? If the idea of four years of mounting debt makes you queasy, you can definitely turn to a community college for a quality education. Why? For one thing, it's typically inexpensive, yet it offers many of the same classes as the larger institutions. Also, you'll probably find a community college that's close to home, so you won't have a room-and-board expense. If you still have your heart set on going to a larger college but don't want to break the bank, consider taking your general requirements on the local level, then transferring the credits to the university of your choice. (Note: Be sure to find out first if your intended college will accept the credits.)

Don't forget to check out scholarship and financial aid opportunities (yup, community colleges offer this stuff, too).

Making the Final Decision: Quotes from Students Who've Been There, Done That

"One thing to consider is that your interests might change. So does your school have more going for it than just the one major you're interested in right now? I picked a liberal arts school with a ton of majors, instead of a smaller engineering school, and it was the right choice. I didn't end up majoring in engineering, but I still had a lot of options."

—Grace, college freshman

"I was really torn between two schools, and I ended up going to visit them both again, even though I'd visited before I applied (they were both close by). Having a refreshed memory of what both places were like helped me to make up my mind."

—Lucille, college sophomore

"A lot of my friends from my graduating class went to the same two schools, which were right near each other. It was hard to decide on the school I go to, which is a couple of hours away; I really didn't want them all to be having fun without me! That was a big factor in me wanting to go to one of those schools. But in the end, I have been glad to have room to make my own path here and meet new people. I think I've had a fuller experience than maybe my high school friends have."

—Tasha, college sophomore

"For me, financial aid was a major factor in my decision. There were a couple of schools where I thought I could have been happy, but this one went way out of its way to make sure I would be able to attend. That seemed like a good sign."

—Jake, college freshman

"When I was deciding between two schools, a teacher pointed out that the retention rate at one of them was superlow, meaning that a lot of students left after their first year. The other school had a decent retention rate. To me, that said that students were getting what they expected . . . so that's where I chose to go."

—Colin, college freshman

"I got into a great and very prestigious school where my parents really wanted me to go. It seemed like a fine place, but I didn't feel any connection to it. Coming to visit this school, though, I immediately started picturing myself on campus, not just going to school here but living, too."

—Lucas, college freshman

"My family and teachers and everyone had a lot of helpful advice, but everyone thought I should do something different! Ultimately, I had to just trust my gut and know that I would make the right decision for myself. No one else could make it."

—Kaela, college freshman

"I got rejected by my top college, where I so wanted to go. I think it was probably a good thing, though. It made me realize how much I had been banking on things going a certain way, and when they didn't, I had to consider some other possibilities. It was good to realize that I could be totally happy in another setting, and I have been."

—Anh, college sophomore

"I went ahead and applied to a couple of crazy expensive schools, even though we couldn't afford them and I didn't think the financial aid would be enough. Fortunately, one of them was willing to negotiate with me and matched the package another school was offering so I wouldn't have any extra costs out of pocket."

—Aaron, college freshman

"After I knew how all of my applications had come out, I sat down and made a list of the most important things I wanted in a college. Then I used that to rank my choices and think about what I wanted. I was surprised at how much that had changed, even just in the time since I sent in the applications."

Nora, college freshman

Preparing for Your First Semester

You're In! What Next?

You've made your decision. You know which school you are going to. Now what? Well, finishing high school is definitely top of the list! But there are some other college-related things you are going to have to take care of now. Here's a list of all your next steps from here to graduation:

- ✓ After you make your final decision, notify the other colleges that accepted you to inform them that you will be attending another college.

✓ Have all your financial issues in order. If you are receiving aid, taking out loans, getting a scholarship, or however you are planning to pay for college, make sure everything is ready and finalized.

✓ Send the tuition deposit to reserve your place in the incoming class.

✓ Fill out all of the housing forms from the residential life office and return them as soon as possible. Most colleges require first-year students to live on campus, but there may be other options. As a freshman, you may have to fill out a questionnaire so that the residential life office can match you with your roommate(s).

✓ Select a meal plan. Most colleges offer options that include the more traditional cafeteria, as well as other eateries on or off campus.

✓ Keep studying. Your acceptance to college is conditional upon good final grades!

✓ Remember to make sure that your high school sends your final transcript to the college of your choice.

✓ Prepare to take the AP exams in May and have the scores sent to your college.

✓ Find out if your college accepts your AP credits or transfer credits from college courses before you arrive on campus in the fall.

Your Parents Are About to Be Empty Nesters!

High hopes for you versus fear for your safety . . . pride over the big step you're about to take and sadness about your taking that step and leaving the nest . . . the desire to help you get into the best college possible but not wanting to overstep the boundaries. These are just a few of the conflicting thoughts that your parents might be having. Applying to college can be an emotional roller coaster for you and your parents.

How do they cope? Some pay attention to every minute detail of your college search and application process, trying to control everything. Some may not want to get involved at all—except to ask, "Which college am I dropping you off at next August?" Most parents fall somewhere in between the two extremes. Even so, your relationship with them is bound to run into a few bumps during this time.

How do YOU cope? Have a heart-to-heart with your parents about your feelings. Don't be afraid to tell them if you need a bit more (or less) support. Then be specific with some things that they might do to make a change. Try to appreciate their perspective. After all, facing the "empty nest" is a big change for them, too!

Contact Your Roommate at Least Once before You Head Off to College

Whether it's by phone, email, or social networking site get acquainted so you'll know what to expect. Stressing over what to say during that first phone call to your new roomie? You know, the total stranger you'll be living with? Here are a few conversation starters to get you past that awkward feeling:

- "Do you know what your major is?"
- "What type of music are you into?"
- "Are you an early bird or a night owl?"
- "Are you thinking of joining any clubs on campus?"

If you hit it off right away, great! If not, don't worry about it. Most friendships take time to develop. And remember, you don't have to be best friends to share a room. Here are some things you can start thinking about, though, as you plan your arrival at your new crib:

- Discuss what to share with your roommate so you don't double up: a telephone, TV, mini-fridge, microwave, vacuum, radio, etc.
- If you can, find out the layout of your room and what kind of furniture is provided so you'll know how big (or small) it is. This way you can figure out how much to bring.
- Find out what appliances your college prohibits. You don't want to lug a mini-fridge all that way only to find your parents have to lug it back home, or you just have to sell it or throw it away!
- Do you and your roommate want to coordinate your decorating styles?

What You'll Need to Bring with You

Whether it's your favorite teddy bear or your funky new flip-flops, be forewarned, you will forget something. Use this checklist to remember important stuff you'll need for dorm life.

- ✓ Extra-long sheets (the regular ones won't fit the extra-long beds)
- ✓ Blankets, quilts, and pillows
- ✓ Towels and washcloths
- ✓ Toiletries
- ✓ Shower caddy (to carry your toiletries to the communal bathroom)
- ✓ Bathrobe (to cover yourself as you walk to and from the communal bathroom)
- ✓ Flip-flops (to use in the shower stalls of the communal bathroom)
- ✓ Iron and ironing board
- ✓ Desk lamp
- ✓ Alarm clock

- ✓ Bulletin board, thumbtacks, stapler, tape, and sticky notes
- ✓ Calendar
- ✓ Posters and pictures for your walls
- ✓ Pencils, pens, and highlighters
- ✓ Extension cords, surge protectors, and batteries
- ✓ Full-length mirror
- ✓ Clothes and hangers
- ✓ A few dishes, cups, and containers
- ✓ Quarters and laundry supplies (including a hamper or laundry bag)
- ✓ Pots and pans (if you're not enrolled in a meal plan)
- ✓ Computer, printer, MP3 player, and all the cables and chargers that go with them!
- ✓ Camera

How to Choose a Computer

All colleges offer educational pricing plans on computers and software. Buy what you can afford, but remember that the top-of-the-line computers are often better quality and may have better warranties.

The majority of students opt for a laptop—easy to take to class, the library, or the local coffeehouse. A lot of colleges offer a wireless option, so you will be able to access the network from various spots on campus with a laptop. Some students may prefer a desktop computer, which can offer more upgradeable options for graphics. Desktops are also much cheaper.

If you can, get a printer, too; that way you don't have to depend on the campus computer center for your printing needs.

When deciding on a PC over a Macintosh or vice versa, take a look at the college network and computer clusters

145

before you buy your computer. You will want a computer that is compatible with the rest of the campus.

In terms of software, you'll definitely want an office suite like Microsoft Office, which includes a word processor (Word), a spreadsheet program (Excel), and sometimes a presentation program (PowerPoint). If you don't get a package with your computer, you can possibly get a college student discount to buy one. There are also free word processing program options like Open Office and Google Docs that you can download online. If you do decide on these programs, make sure to save documents in rich text format (.rtf). This format is the only one that will work well when submitting documents to professors. Also, purchase virus protection software—campus networks are rife with viruses! In fact, your college may offer virus software for free.

One of the advantages of a college campus is that computers are available in almost every building, so make sure that you purchase at least one flash drive to carry your work around with you.

Note: Once you're in college, your exposure on social networking sites increases. New peers and professors, as well as your resident advisor and even that creepy kid from down the hall, may be looking at your sites. So keep up that online housecleaning!

Regular Phone versus Cell Phone

Telecommunications plans vary from college to college, so be very careful to find out the specifics of yours when you arrive on campus. Some colleges do not charge additional fees for basic telephone service in the dorms, while at others only on-campus calls are free, so you'd have to purchase a package of some kind.

While cell phones may be more expensive than a regular phone provided by the college, there is no question that the majority of students are using them to stay in touch with each other. Cell phones are also more versatile, allowing students to send text messages, email, and photos. More and more companies are wooing families with teenage and college-age students by offering "family plans" with unlimited minutes within a defined user group and unlimited text messaging. If your parents are paying for your phone, you should discuss this issue with them before you come to a final decision.

Orientation

This is the time (usually a few weeks before classes begin) to get a feel for the campus and to meet others in your graduating class. What will you do?

- Learn how to get around campus.
- Stay in the dorm with roommates for a couple of nights.
- Participate in fun "freshman bonding" activities.
- Register for your first classes.

Here are some tips on how to make the most of your freshman orientation:

- Be friendly and TALK to people. Join a game of Frisbee or Hacky Sack, or start your own. Hang out with your orientation roomies and the other people on your floor. You'll be glad to have a few friendly faces to call up when you officially arrive for school.
- Find your classrooms, the laundry room, and the cafeteria.
- Go over the course catalog, and make a list of classes that you'd like to take. Make sure you have alternates when you go to register. Being a freshman, you may not get your first choices (or your second ones).
- Explore the area around campus—check out shopping, restaurants, and the landscape where you'll be spending the next four years.

First-Semester Fees

Guess what? Tuition does NOT cover everything. Sure, it's a big part of your expense, but it's the little things that can catch you off guard.

In addition to tuition and room and board, plan on spending your dough on the following:

- Course-related fees
- Student services fees
- Health insurance fees
- On-campus parking fees if you have a car
- Books and supplies. Don't be surprised if you find yourself paying hundreds of dollars for your Psych 101 textbook and the highlighters you'll need to mark important passages. Reduce book expenses significantly by buying gently used texts instead of brand spankin' new ones. Additionally, consider renting the textbook from either the bookstore or online. You can even ask your professor if you can use a much cheaper copy of the textbook's last edition.
- Personal items. You'll be forking over big bucks on toiletries, laundry stuff, clothes, phone bills, movies, trips home, midnight pizza runs, and more.

Banking

This may or may not be the first time you open a checking or savings account. If it is, here are some tips on picking a bank to trust with your moola.

- "Location! Location! Location!" Choose a bank that has branches near campus and your hometown.
- Ask an upperclassman for bank advice.
- Look for low- or no-minimum balance requirements.
- Use no-fee ATMs whenever possible.

- If your parents are going to be making deposits to another bank, give them electronic transfer information or deposit slips/envelopes.
- If you have savings, find a CD or money market account for higher interest earnings. Don't forget to consider credit unions. They are essentially the same as banks, except they may be specifically geared towards helping students such as yourself.

Debit versus Credit Cards

Credit card or debit card? BE MONEY SMART and understand the advantages and risks of each.

When you use a credit card, you're incurring debt. You can either pay the balance off immediately or pay it off over a period of time, with interest charged. When you use a debit card, funds are debited from your checking or savings account connected to the card.

Good Things about Credit Cards

- Convenient. You don't have to carry cash or checks and you pay later.
- No PIN. A transaction, unless getting a cash advance, does not require a personal identification number (PIN).
- Not connected to your personal account. The funds paying for your transaction are those of a lender, so if a crook goes on a spending spree with your card, your personal banking accounts aren't affected.
- Liability in merchant disputes. You can dispute a transaction if it goes sour.
- Liability for unauthorized transactions. If your card is lost or stolen and used, you are only liable for $50—even if you don't notice it for 90 days.
- Along with student loans, it's the easiest way to form a credit history, which is really important nowadays.

notify

149

- It's awesome if you're ever in an emergency and you're out of cash.
- Hey, they might even give you a free T-shirt for applying!

Bad Things about Credit Cards

- Charging stuff is, in essence, a loan. It's borrowing money. If you don't pay off that bill at the end of the month, you'll have to pay interest on that loan (probably at a hefty rate!).
- If you miss a payment or two, your interest rate will skyrocket even more.
- If you keep charging and not paying, after four years, you'll end up owing big on a student loan AND a credit card.
- Bad payment practices in college can ruin your credit history before it even begins.
- If you are under 21, you will need a parent signature to apply for a card. No parent signature and you will have to wait!
- Applying for a credit card does not guarantee you receive one. However, the school's bank or credit union tend to be the most likely to approve you for a card.

Good Things about Debit Cards

- Convenient. You don't have to carry cash or checks.
- No debt! You can only spend what's in your account.
- A debit card takes a PIN, which provides an extra layer of protection.
- Liability for unauthorized transactions. More and more banks are protecting debit card owners from liability for unauthorized transactions. Check your bank's policies on this.

Bad Things about Debit Cards

- It's connected to your personal account, so if you spend too much, you'll get hefty overdraft charges, on top of the fact that you've run out of money!
- Liability for unauthorized transactions. Some banks may not cover your losses if your card is stolen and used.

Staying Out of Debt

As if by magic, becoming a college freshman will suddenly make you an attractive credit card candidate, even though you have no way to pay the bills. You're out there now, free to roam and purchase to your heart's content. It is SO easy to dig yourself into a big pit of debt. So watch out! Don't get over your head in debt. To keep it in check:

- Search for a company that gives you a low interest rate and apply for the card with the best deal.
- Try to pay cash avoid using your credit card, except in emergencies.
- Before buying, ask, "Do I really need this? Is this an emergency?" If the answer is something like, "I'll DIE if I don't get these extra cheesy nachos," don't charge it.
- Before charging, ask, "Can I pay this off in a month?" If the answer is no, reconsider.
- Learn how to balance a checking account and read a bank statement.
- Don't miss a credit card payment—your interest rate will skyrocket! If you did mistakenly spend more than you can pay, make sure to pay at least the monthly minimum balance to avoid disaster.

Bad payment practices in college will ruin your blossoming credit history, which can affect future loans and jobs.

Homeowner's Insurance

"When you're away at college, is your stuff covered by our homeowner's insurance?" your parents may ask you. The answer is complicated! If you're a full-time college student, your parents' insurance generally provides some coverage in a dorm, possibly with other limits for electronics like PCs and TVs. If you live off campus, some companies don't provide coverage at all, and some don't if the apartment is rented in your name only. In that case, you may decide to buy renter's insurance. Bottom line: consult your parents' insurance agent.

And, hey, to guard against theft on campus:

- Always lock doors. If you're going down the hall to the bathroom or to chat with friends, you should lock the door, and keep the keys with you. *keep it to yourself*
- Leave expensive jewelry and irreplaceables at home. Don't risk losing fine jewelry or other sentimental items to a thief.
- Engrave electronic items. Computers, TVs, and MP3 players should be engraved with your driver's license number and the state in which you live. This helps police track stolen articles.
- Don't leave belongings unattended on campus. A backpack left unguarded in the library is a quick, easy target for thieves.

Source: Insurance Information Institute, Inc.

Financial To-Dos

Money may not be the root of all evil, but managing it responsibly can sure be a challenge! Maybe you are already a savvy saver and a selective spender; if not, it's time to begin learning about financial independence:

- Ask your parents for a clear discussion of expectations (on both sides) for spending, budgeting, and money emergencies.
- Build a budget for books and supplies, student fees, snacks, toiletries, phone bills, dry cleaning, entertainment, haircuts, on-campus parking, trips home, and extras.
- Call your insurance agent to investigate your health, car, and homeowner's insurance policies.
- Pick your bank (see section on banks).
- Get a credit or debit card and discuss limits with your folks.
- Practice using an ATM, writing checks, and doing online banking before you get on campus.
- Research whether your school offers seminars or information on money management.
- Investigate the best place to put your savings or work-study paychecks.
- Consider getting a part-time job that offers an employee discount.
- Buy gently used textbooks.
- Opt for the college's meal plan—at least for freshman year. Then dining will be one out-of-pocket expense you won't have to worry about.
- Ask for student freebies and discounts at restaurants, theaters, airlines, and museums!
- Explore free entertainment that you can do with your friends: concerts and athletics, working out at the college sports complex, hanging out in the quad, etc. Hang out on campus—most college activities are free or close to it!

Did you know a huge percentage of today's students are taking responsibility for part of college expenses? Over 65 percent of Bachelor's degree recipients graduate in debt, averaging more than $23,000.

Finding a Doctor

Your college's student health center is a great starting place for health and wellness questions or problems. At most schools, the student health center provides free or low-cost basic health care for undergrads, including checkups and treatment for routine illnesses and injuries. They can also give you a referral to a local doctor if you need further care.

If you are covered by your parents' insurance, take a look at the insurance provider's website. Most will offer a "find a doctor" option that lets you search based on a doctor's specialty, gender, or distance from you—and when you find a doctor this way, you know you won't need to worry about whether he or she is covered by your insurance!

Dealing with Homesickness

You might get a little homesick at college—even if you couldn't WAIT to get out of town. It's only natural to feel a little stressed about being away from family and friends for the first time. Here are some tips on what to do and not to do:

What to Do

- Call your parents or your siblings. They'll be glad to hear from you!

- Talk to your resident advisor (RA). He or she will be sympathetic and can probably help you get through homesickness, as well as any stress or confusion you may be experiencing.

- If you feel comfortable, talk to your roommate about it, or plan a fun activity together to help build the friendship.

- Keep in touch with friends from home, but don't get upset if your best bud is having the time of her life. Everybody adjusts differently to a new environment.

- Get involved in a club or activity. It's the best way to meet new people and to feel more comfortable on campus.

- Research the Greek lifestyle on campus. If you decide to rush and are accepted into a fraternity or sorority, you can enjoy a built-in support system to help you through college and a bunch of lifelong friends!

What Not to Do

- Don't feel embarrassed about a tough adjustment.

- Don't go straight to your room after class. Hang out in the quad, take a swim at the sports complex, anything!

- Don't isolate yourself from making new friends. If someone asks if you want to grab a latte after class, say yes!

It your transition blues seem to get worse as the semester progresses, if you can't shake the blues after talking to your parents, friends, or RA, or whatever it is you've been trying to help you feel better, don't wait to get help! Go to the counseling center, or seek out the advice of a spiritual leader. Never forget that you are not alone! There are plenty of people trained to help you through the rough patches.

First Semester To-Dos

- If you can, contact your roommate before you head to college!

- Make sure you have a list of what you'll need! It's the best way to avoid leaving things behind.

- Get the computer situation sorted out

- Figure out if you are going with a landline phone or a cell phone, or both!

- Get your finances in order. Pick your bank and open an account! Also, make sure any first semester fees are taken care of.

- Don't forget to find out what's going on with your homeowner's insurance and health care coverage, and what the health center's services are.

- Register for classes! Pick out your classes right away, and have lists of second and third choices ready. Also, register as early as possible. Most schools have online registration capabilities, which is really great. If your school doesn't, you will likely be joining all the other undergrads in a mad dash to the registrar's office.

- If you find that your homesickness is getting way out of control, don't wait to get help! Don't brush off your feelings. Your health and well-being are the most important things, above everything else.

- Most important, have fun.

Chapter 6:
Social Media and College Admissions

How Social Media Is Altering the College Admissions Process—and How it Can Help OR Hurt Your Chances of Getting In

It's not just an urban legend. It's actually happening. Increasingly, your latest tweets, the photos you've posted on Pinterest, your YouTube antics, your Tumblr posts, your Google Pluses, and your Facebook status updates are showing up on the radar screens of college admissions officers. And many colleges have said that what they've seen isn't doing applicants any favors. So while your SAT or ACT score, GPA, letters of recommendation, and written personal essays are still the most important part of your application, what colleges find along your digital trail can in fact hamstring your admissions chances. In this chapter, you'll read about proprietary research from Kaplan Test Prep on this topic, as well as advice on ways to make sure your admissions chances aren't torpedoed by your online digital footprint.

Here the latest: According to Kaplan Test Prep's 2012 survey of college admissions officers*, schools are increasingly discovering information on Google and Facebook and other social networking sites that are negatively impacting applicants' chances of getting in. While the percentage of admissions officers who took to Google (27%) and checked Facebook and other sites (26%) as part of the applicant review process increased slightly from 2011 (20% for Google and 26% for Facebook), the percentage who said they discovered something that negatively impacted an applicant's chances of getting into the school nearly tripled—from 12% in 2011 to 35% this year. Offenses cited included essay plagiarism, vulgarities in blogs, alcohol consumption in photos, things that made them "wonder," and "illegal activities." (It's all fun and games until your parent or an admissions officer finds out, right?) In 2008, when Kaplan began tracking this trend, only one in 10 admissions officers reported checking applicants' social networking pages.

Before we go any further, let's dispel a few myths on this:

- **Myth: Checking Facebook pages is a wide-spread practice among admissions officers.** It's not. Nearly three-quarters of the schools surveyed said they do not check applicants' Facebook pages. And the 26% who report turning to Facebook say they don't do so as a general rule—for the most part, these schools will do so only if something in the application raises a question mark or causes them to do so. Reasons cited are both positive (scholarship consideration) and negative (suspicion something on the application is untrue). In reality, schools are philosophically divided on whether an applicant's digital trail is fair game, and the majority of admissions officers do not look beyond the submitted application.
- **Myth: I have tight privacy settings on my profile, so no admissions officers can find me or see what I post.** Anecdotal evidence from Kaplan's survey suggests that some students are sabotaging others at the admissions office. Admissions officers reported receiving anonymous tips pointing them to digital dirt on applicants. Think about it—do you know and trust every single one of the hundreds of friends in your Facebook network? Are there competitive classmates, ex-boyfriends or girlfriends, frenemies or people you've never actually met face-to-face with access to your Facebook

posts? It's hard to believe, but welcome to the "Mean Girls" era: your Facebook trail may not be as private as you think.

- **Myth: I don't have a Facebook page, so this isn't even an issue for me. (Or, I changed my Facebook name so admissions officers won't be able to find me.)** Guess what? Today it's all about Google. In Kaplan's survey, the trend line for using Google is steeper than for Facebook - and Google will turn up YouTube videos, Tumblr posts, Tweets, Flickr photos, Pinterest boards, Google+ profiles, blogs. We're in an era with a plethora of social channels for sharing comments, observations, opinions, photos and videos with the touch of a button—and content on many of these new channels can be easily found using search engines like Google, Bing, and Yahoo. It may not be your Facebook post—but the photos your friends tagged you in, the mention of you in your teammate's Tumblr posts, the heat-of-the-moment expletive you Tweeted, the opinions you shared on video.

By the way, if you think you're safe once you get into college—think again. Kaplan also surveyed admissions officers at graduate schools, business schools and law schools and found a significant number also find content along applicants' trails that negatively impact their admissions chances. Of the nearly half (!) of law school admissions officers who checked an applicant's digital trail, 28% said what they found negatively impacted an applicant. Of the one-third of business schools who took to Google, Facebook or other social networking sites, 10% found something that negatively impacted an applicant. And of the 15% of graduate school admissions officers surveyed who reported checking on applicants online, 12% found something that negatively impacted an applicant.

Why the explosion in finding content deemed as "objectionable"? Three key reasons: growing acceptance of the Internet as a resource by college admissions officers, the ongoing proliferation (yes, that's an SAT word) of social media sites and the rise of a generation used to sharing online.

Growing Acceptance of the Internet as a Resource

When Kaplan first began surveying college admissions officers on the use of social media in the evaluation process, just about one in ten had checked an applicant's Facebook (or, at the time, MySpace) profile. But savvy admissions officers have always recognized that the traditional pieces of the application show the "polished" version of an applicant: essays have been rewritten several times and reviewed by others, letters of recommendation whose writers have been fully screened.

Just a few years ago, an admissions officer might pick up the phone and call a guidance counselor or reference to get additional background. Today, some of that additional color can be found online with a simple Internet search—and often what's found is the "raw" unedited version: photos of you tagged by your friends, the opinionated tweets you posted about a current events issue, the Pinterest board you created of your favorite things. In fact, what's found online may not even have been something you posted. Are you an athlete? A quick search will likely turn up your name with sports stats. Were you ever in a sponsored competitive event, like a science fair or spelling bee? Chances are your name is on the sponsor's web site. Were you ever in the local paper? Every publication now posts its articles online. A few years ago, many admissions officers considered "looking up a student online" to be synonymous with checking Facebook profiles and were uncomfortable with the notion. Today "looking up a student online" means picking up additional color about a student from a range of publicly available sources—which for many schools feels more acceptable.

Over the past few years, schools have also taken to using social media and the Internet for recruiting purposes – 87% of schools surveyed are using Facebook, Twitter and other channels to promote themselves to candidates. Five years ago, few schools had Facebook pages; today, almost all do. To be clear, there's a big difference between colleges using social media for recruiting purposes versus using it to check applicants' profiles. But the explosion in social media use among colleges and universities for recruiting shows that schools are getting used to the idea of using the Internet in some way as part of the admissions process.

Ongoing Proliferation of Social Media Sites

What else is causing the increase in "objectionable" material found online? The dramatic increase in new social media sites. Jeff Olson, Kaplan Test Prep's vice president of data science notes, "For years, social media was a one-platform trend—first it was Friendster, then it was MySpace, then Facebook. But today's social media landscape has proliferated to include Twitter, YouTube, Pinterest, Instagram, Tumblr, Flickr and so many other platforms—and teens today are using all of these channels." Granted, some channels flame out as quickly as the latest fashion trends, but with so many options and with teens always shifting to what's new, a lot of digital content lives on, on forgotten or abandoned profiles.

A Generation Used to Sharing

Today's teens have grown up with a very fluid sense of privacy norms, and there are at least two drivers: technology and cultural mindset. Back in the day, teens wrote down personal thoughts and opinions in diaries and journals which were usually locked in a drawer or hidden under a mattress. Today, the leather journals and snap-lock diaries have been replaced by Facebook,

Tumblr, YouTube, Twitter. Enabling technologies (smartphones, Webcams, tablets) and apps make sharing easier. Spotify will share what songs your friends are listening to, Foursquare will share where they're hanging out, Instagram will share what they're taking pictures of—all with a few finger taps. And in an age where celebrities and politicians tweet personal photos and "reality" shows are a dime a dozen, sharing personal information is a cultural norm for most American teens. For today's teens, snapping a picture and posting it comes as naturally as eating and sleeping.

Add to this mix, the fact that most admissions staff are from that previous generation that kept personal thoughts private. Most admissions counselors grew up before Facebook even existed. If they had Internet, it was this slow thing that the whole family would share from one computer. There is a generation gap between some of them and the culture that you have grown up within, and this can sometimes lead to miscommunications.

In the face of all these trends, the rise in discovery of digital dirty laundry is inevitable.

What Does All This Mean for College Admissions?

Good and bad news: schools are still figuring things out. Kaplan's survey also found that only 15% of colleges currently have rules regarding the checking of applicants' Facebook or social networking pages—a percentage that has remained fairly consistent over the past few years. Of schools that do have a policy, 69% said the policy prohibited admissions officers from visiting applicants' pages. But this still means the vast majority of admissions officers (85% of colleges have no policies, and 31% of schools with policies do not prohibit checking) have the flexibility to act at their own discretion. As noted earlier, it's not standard practice.

(Said one admissions officer: "Do we ever do this? Yes. As a general rule? No." while another noted: "It's not a regular part of the process, but it's admissible.") And colleges are not jumping to set policies on checking students' digital trails—the low percentage of schools with policies hasn't changed meaningfully from when Kaplan first surveyed admissions officers about this in 2008. Bottom line: think of this as the "Wild, Wild West" of the admissions process.

What Should I Do?

So before you panic, following are a few simple steps to follow.

- **Check your digital trail regularly and keep it clean.** Search yourself on Google, Bing, Yahoo and other search engines, while not logged in as yourself , and clean up anything that doesn't put you in a positive light. You may be surprised by what comes up. If that means asking a friend or an acquaintance to take something down that they posted about you, do it.

- **Get to know your privacy settings.** When you set up an account with any social media channel, assume that the default setting is for anything you post to be completely public. It is up to you to change your profile settings. For Facebook, set your privacy to limit who can view your posts, and request to review anything you're tagged in. For Google+, set up your circles so that only people you know well and trust can see your personal posts. For Twitter, change your Tweet Privacy to Protected. For YouTube, keep your videos private (you can limit to 25 viewers) or set them to "Unlisted" when posting. For Pinterest, post your private or personal photos only to your Secret Boards (every user gets three); everything else you post on

Pinterest is public. We can go on and on—but just make sure for every new channel you join, assume what you post is public and findable until you take the time to set your privacy otherwise. *(Note: Social media sites' privacy settings change on a relatively frequent basis, so always make sure to know what's current.)*

- **Only share with people you know and trust.** The hottie whose pic you saw in your friend's network? The cool guy/girl you met once at a party? Your brother's teammate who you have a crush on? The friend of a friend who reportedly has a connection to Rihanna? They may be cool to have in your network—but would you actually hand them a journal with your private thoughts? Trust them with your wallet? Unless you know they'd be willing to put themselves on the line for you, there's no reason anyone beyond your closest friends and family would feel the need to keep your information private—and you have no idea who they're connected or related to. So you can either make sure people you don't know well don't have access to your personal posts—or don't connect with them at all. (Your third option is to never post anything you wouldn't want a college admissions officer or future employer to see. Yeah, this would be hard and limiting for most of us; at the same time, social networks are niceties not necessities.)

- **Keep your social media profile photos appropriate.** Even if you set your privacy settings so you're searchable but only friends can see your posts and pictures, your name and profile photo are still visible. If so, make sure your photo is what you want to present if someone pulls up your profile.

- **Take control of tagging on your profile.** Facebook's default settings allow friends to tag you in their photos, profile posts, and even check you into places—which can be public without your knowledge. Change these settings so only friends can see these posts. You can also choose to review all tags before they are linked to your profile so that your friends don't have the chance to link embarrassing party photos without your permission.

- **Avoid posts from mobile sites.** Increasingly, social network sites are providing the ability to post updates from your cell phone. While this allows you to send quick updates on the run, it can also lead to less choice on where your post is sent. You might also think less thoroughly regarding potential posts. Worst of all, its sometime impossible to erase a post from your phone even if you immediately realize it was a mistake.

Most importantly: Think before you Tweet (or post). You don't have to share everything with everyone. After all your hard work, the last thing you want to keep you out of your top school or program choices is an inappropriate Facebook status update, Instagram or Pinterest photo or offensive tweet. Even bragging on your profile that a school is your "safety" school can come back to bite you. (According to Kaplan's research, it has!)

So we've spent some time talking about how social media sites and the Internet can negatively impact your college admissions chances. But on the flip slide, in can positively impact your admission chances. College and universities love talented, passionate students, so showing them your passions may improve your chances of getting in. Here are some examples:

- Are you a talented artist? If so, why not create a web site where you can show off your portfolio of work? That's how a site like Pinterest, for

[auditorily
visually

example, can be helpful. Be sure to include the link in your college application.

- Are you an athlete? Consider creating a YouTube channel with videos of your winning moments.
- Do you write for your school's newspaper? Create a page where you can post the best articles you've written.
- Do you love to write short stories and poems? Why not create a blog where you can showcase your most inspiring work?
- If you are a passionate photographer, Tumblr's photo blogs might be the perfect venue for your most beautiful, inspiring images.
- Are you a would be Mozart or pop star? Upload videos and recording to YouTube or your page hosted another site to showcase your talent.

A word of caution: Whatever you are posting, make sure it's accurate and honest. While it's fine to do a little "humble bragging" about your accomplishments, don't lie or embellish them.

While the vast majority of colleges are not playing online versions of Sherlock Holmes or Veronica Mars, almost all are using some kind of social media to recruit students. These percentages have increased steadily since Kaplan began tracking the issue.

87% use Facebook
76% use Twitter
73% use YouTube

Some advice on interacting with colleges on social media:

- It's perfectly acceptable and even encouraged to "like" a school's official page, but don't send a friend request to an admissions officer's personal page. Think that's unusual? Previous

> Kaplan research has found most admissions officers have received a friend request from an applicant.
>
> - Twitter can be a terrific source of digestible news and info about the school, in 140 characters or less. So follow the school's official Twitter feed, but not the admissions officer's personal Twitter feed.
>
> - And YouTube can feature everything from interviews with alumni and professors to campus tours. (That said, nothing takes the place of an in-person campus tour.)

All this explained, keep the following in perspective.

- In the grand scheme of things, your online brand plays a relatively small role in the admissions process. It's the wild card. It may help you or it may hurt you. But to what extent it does, really depends on what the content is and the subjectivity of the admissions officer.

- Admissions officers see thousands of applications every year. There is no way they can do online research about every applicant.

- Those who told us they have done it don't do it all the time—in fact it's probably something they do for a small percentage of applicants.

- At the end of the day, it's going to be the traditional factors that determine whether you get in or not: your SAT or ACT sores, GPA, letters of recommendation, personal essays and extracurricular activities.

Some parting words on this topic: Be smart and think about everything you share digitally before you do it… and not just because you think a college admissions officer might see it. If you wouldn't be comfortable posting something on a billboard in front of your high school, under your name, it's probably not a good idea to post it online. At least a billboard can't be passed around and can get taken down. Digital footprints can be easily shared and can last a very long time. Don't let a momentary lapse of judgement leave a lasting online impression!

*Kaplan Test Prep's 2012 survey of college admission officers was conducted by phone between July and September 2012 and included responses from admissions officers at 350 of the top 500 colleges and universities – as ranked by U.S. News & World Report.

Index